The Sober Entrepreneur

RUSS PERRY

Copyright @ 2017 by Russ Perry. All rights reserved.

Published in the United States by Insurgent Publishing, LLC.
PO Box 8043, Aspen, CO 81612
www.insurgentpublishing.com

No part of this publication may be reproduced, stored in a retrieval system, or transmitted, in any form or by any means, electronic, mechanical, photocopying, recording, or otherwise, in whole or in part, without written permission from the publisher, except in the case of brief quotations embodied in critical reviews and certain other non-commercial uses permitted by copyright law. For permission requests, please email the publisher at admin@insurgentpublishing.com.

Ordering Information:

Insurgent Publishing books are available at special discounts for bulk purchases for sales promotions or corporate use. Special editions, including personalized covers, excerpts of existing books, or books with corporate logos, can be created in large quantities upon request. For more information, please contact the publisher by email at admin@insurgentpublishing.com.

Although every precaution has been taken to verify the accuracy of the information contained herein, the author and publisher assume no responsibility for any errors or omissions. No liability is assumed for damages that may result from the use of information contained within.

Publisher's Cataloging-in-Publication Data

Names: Perry, Russ.
Title: The Sober Entrepreneur / Russ Perry.
Description: Aspen, CO : Insurgent Publishing, 2016. l Includes bibliographical references.
ISBN 978-1-940715-06-3 (pbk.) l ISBN 978-1-940715-07-0 (hardcover)

Printed in the United States of America

10 9 8 7 6 5 4 3 2 1

Need more help getting sober?

I wrote this book to help as many people as possible beat the bottle (or any addiction that's taking over your life).

This book is a good start.

But if you want access to additional resources, please go to:

soberentrepreneur.com/bonus

This page will be updated from time to time with resources that are helping me, and that I believe could help you.

Thanks, and stay strong.

- Russ

*For Mika, Maddix, Reese, and Paige.
I love you! #PTTT*

If no one else has ever told you this before, I will tell it to you one more time and hope you believe it and never forget it for the rest of your life: You deserve to be treated well.

– Andrew W.K.

CONTENTS

Foreword	1
Introduction	4
Chapter One: Breaking Point	9
Chapter Two: We All Have Problems	23
Chapter Three: Sedation Is the Enemy	44
Chapter Four: Addicted to the Hustle	56
Chapter Five: Beat the Block	68
Chapter Six: Scarcity	80
Chapter Seven: Who's on Your Boat?	104
Chapter Eight: A Year of Firsts	127
Chapter Nine: The Four-Part Upgrade	144
Chapter Ten: Bringing It Home	191

The Sober Entrepreneur

FOREWORD

By Peter Shankman

I decided to quit drinking on October 29th, 2015. There was no real "reason." Drinking hadn't impacted my work. It hadn't really impacted my relationships. I wasn't arrested or anything like that. I simply decided that I was better off without alcohol, so I quit.

In the last few years, I've talked to a lot of people who've quit drinking. The majority of them say that quitting was a process. It took them a while, they needed to be ready, they had some sort of major impact in their lives that forced them to do it. Their spouse left them. They got arrested. They had to wear an ankle bracelet. Tons and tons of reasons. Very few of them just woke up one day and decided to quit.

The ones who did, though? The ones who said "I'm going to quit drinking" as nonchalantly as you'd say

"I'm going to have a slice of pizza?" They were, by far, all entrepreneurs.

See, entrepreneurs, as I tell all my friends, tend to have only two speeds: "Namaste," and "I'll cut a bitch." We don't moderate. Moderation is for losers. We're all or nothing, every single time.

While that attitude is great for business, and has certainly helped me get to where I am in my professional life, there can be negative repercussions in other areas. "Leftover pizza," for instance, isn't a thing for people like us. Neither is "a light 5k run." Nope, we're going from sitting on our couch to doing an Ironman Triathlon in under a year. And of course, we don't have just one drink. We have ten.

Sobriety in entrepreneurship is an undiscussed modus operandi, but one that we're seeing more and more. To be at the top of your game, you can't have distractions. And the biggest distraction comes from not truly knowing yourself. Once you begin to, everything changes, usually for the better.

My friend Russ has written a brutally raw and honest book about how he changed himself and the ups and the downs that went along with it, and I'm honored to write the foreword for it.

None of us know what the future will bring. But I do know that when I quit drinking, the future got surprisingly brighter — even if it was only slightly dim for me to begin with.

Enjoy this book. May it help you to get where you want to be.

Peter Shankman
Shankman.com
August 3, 2017

INTRODUCTION

On October 22nd, 2013, I stopped drinking. In the two years prior to that decision, my marriage had been one step away from catastrophe, and my business had just about burned down. It's not an exaggeration to say that my life as I knew it hung in the balance — I could keep drinking, or I could stay married. I couldn't have it both ways. So on a quiet Sunday, alcohol and I parted ways for good.

The decision to stop drinking was mine alone. It didn't come from my wife or business partners. It didn't come from my family or anyone else in my life. It all came down to a realization deep within myself that I was at a crossroads, and that this was the most important decision I would ever make in my life.

At the time, I never thought I'd be writing a book about the decision. There was so much in my life that needed immediate attention, and it would be years until the idea even surfaced. But when it did finally pop into my head, I knew I wanted to do it… and then I spent the better part of a year trying to wrangle my thoughts and experiences into something that would be useful. I was on the cusp of giving up on the whole project when, in the course of a single week, four different men reached out to me to discuss their paths to sobriety.

They were all successful married men who had built entrepreneurial businesses, and they were all struggling with alcohol in their own ways. During conversations with these men and other guys just like them, it became obvious that many entrepreneurs need a resource that will help them identify where they have opportunities to change for the better, and will help them start down their path to sobriety.

Entrepreneurs are often all-or-nothing types. We're either "on", going a thousand miles an hour, or we're "off"… but the "off" setting can be hard to reach without "a little something" to calm us down. We're highly risk-tolerant, and we work with an intensity most people will never experience. That's a powerful combination, but also a dangerous one. It can create multi-million dollar businesses, and it can create crippling isolation. To create something remarkable, we develop a drive and focus that can alienate or scare other people, and so we often end up on the road alone.

Isolation is at the core of addictive behaviors, and while this book focuses on alcohol particularly, addictions come in all shapes and sizes. I've seen men addicted to their work, casual sex, overeating, pain killers, pornography, hard drugs, and various other extreme behaviors, like BASE jumping or racing motorbikes — anything that will make them feel *something*. As you read this book, feel free to substitute "alcohol" with the challenges you're currently facing, and don't let the specifics blind you to the greater message: if you're isolating yourself, self-medicating, or habitually taking huge, unnecessary risks, you have a problem.

Whatever your particular *thing* is, if you're an entrepreneur with extreme tendencies, this book is for you. Right now, the majority of resources around addiction are academic, or they're doom-and-gloom programs designed to intercept people one step away from homelessness. This book is not like those. You will not find fluffy, theoretical self-help advice, nor will you get a heavy, self-righteous lecture on why you must absolve yourself of all your indulgences. I'm not here to moralize — I'm here to show you how quitting your addiction will help you kick ass in your personal life and in your business too.

Tim Ferriss is one of my favorite authors. He created

an incredible way of getting things done with hacks and shortcuts, popularizing the term "lifestyle design" — the conscious process of building the life you really want. Getting sober is the *ultimate* in lifestyle design, but despite my admiration for his work (and the work of many others he has inspired), I've yet to see conversations on how to optimize your life with an addiction and family in tow. This book is designed to fill that gap.

Now, no book can replace the programs that have been around for decades, designed to directly tackle the issues of addiction and high-risk behavior. I am not a doctor, therapist, psychologist, or hypnotist, and am not professionally qualified to give out psychological diagnoses or treatment plans. This book is simply a collection of my experiences, opinions, and the results I've had. Having been to both, I recommend Alcoholics Anonymous (AA) or Celebrate Recovery. They are great programs for proven support at any stage, and a quick Google search can find you a meeting, today, nearby.

If you have thought about (or are considering) suicide, please talk to someone immediately. In my darkest times, I was isolated, scared, and afraid. Addiction makes us feel alone, and the only way out of the hole is to connect with someone. Know you're *not* alone — you will pull through this, and the only thing you need to do right now is to make that phone call. If you don't feel comfortable reaching out to someone in your life, please call the National Suicide Prevention Hotline at +1-800-273-8255 to speak to someone who understands what you're going through. It's free and confidential.

For all the men who have thought once, twice, a hundred times, "Maybe I should quit drinking" — this book is also for you. We'll begin with my personal journey: how going sober radically transformed my business, saved my marriage, and overhauled my health. You'll get all the frameworks I used to quit and the lessons I learned along the way, so that you can apply them to your own life.

While a journey like this is not easy, it *is* worth it. If you follow this path yourself, you'll certainly be in the minority of people who have taken this level of responsibility for themselves — but the reward on the other side of the bottle is bigger than you could ever imagine.

CHAPTER ONE: BREAKING POINT

Alcohol has been a taboo presence in my life for as long as I can remember. My dad's family was riddled with alcoholism, and his drinking was one of the many wedges that came between my parents and eventually led to their divorce when I was two years old. I can count the times I've seen my mom drink on one hand. She never talked much about alcohol, but when she did the message was clear: alcohol was bad. Growing up without any real exposure to alcohol allowed me to minimize the risks I saw in my dad's behavior, and as I grew up, alcohol started to seem pretty cool.

During high school, I got into all kinds of mischief fuelled by alcohol. Most of my antics slipped past my mom unnoticed, but before I graduated I had already had a run in with the police. By the time I got to college,

I had fully embraced drinking and threw myself into it during my first year. Arizona State University had no shortage of parties and events to fuel the "fun."

This continued well into my adult life, and many of the epic nights of my twenties involved drinking. The first date I ever went on with my wife Mika ended up being a day-long adventure, bouncing from bar to bar in a whirlwind of shots and cocktails. Some of the worst nights of my life also involved drinking. While it wasn't strictly "rock bottom," my drinking career reached a new low the night I woke up in a jail cell in Clark County, Nevada, with no idea how the hell I got there. Turns out I'd been resisting arrest for drunk and disorderly behavior, later defined in the police report as "dancing-like motions."

But the worst night of all came a few years later, when I got caught in an affair.

It was 2011, and Mika and I had been married for a few years. I had been slaving through 14-hour days for years on end, trying to get a creative agency to turn a profit. But I wasn't just working… I was *drinking* and working. If you watched the TV series *Mad Men*, you'll be familiar with the lavish drinking culture associated with media agencies, and while times have changed, the drinking culture has carried on from the 1960s uninterrupted. Beer carts, happy hours, and champagne breakfasts are common practice in the industry, both as a way to keep staff engaged and to woo potential clients with fun indulgences.

I fully embraced the drinking culture of advertising, but drinking eventually became a major conflict of interest with my efforts to make the business profitable. Operations started to erode with my lack of focus, and the reputation of the agency started sliding into a self-inflicted downward spiral. Clients became increasingly frustrated with our services, while I was increasingly frustrated with my situation. One day our biggest client walked away from $40,000 worth of invoices that we delivered over a handshake agreement, and we soon lost two other clients, totaling a loss of over $450,000 in potential revenue. My team mutinied over our pathetic performance, and I realized too late that the whole ship was going down.

Adding to the mounting pressure, Mika was pregnant. For the previous 18 months, my business had often been one decision away from complete bankruptcy, and our financial insecurity became even more terrifying knowing a baby was on the way. Pregnancy should be a joyous time, but I was in a dark place — keeping everything to myself, trying as hard as I could to stay above water. As my friends were getting promotions and buying homes, my wife and I were short-selling our condo and leveraging credit cards to buy Christmas presents.

Drinking was no longer a social activity, but a lifeline. I drank to find an escape, and could be expected to black out after a night (or day) of drinking. I was so stressed I barely recognized myself — a shell of the man my wife had married and not in a fit state to be anyone's father. In this pressure-cooker situation, I hired a woman with experience managing clients to help me rectify the situation at work. I knew I needed to get the business back on track, to start bringing in revenue again so that I could support my growing family. But that growth never happened. I was drowning in the isolation, and destroying myself with heavy drinking. Within a few months the unthinkable happened and I was involved in an affair.

An affair is rarely the result of one big decision. Instead, affairs evolve from hundreds or thousands of small decisions that erode your commitments, common sense, and ethics. Drinking makes it easy to make destructive decisions, as your judgement is severely impaired. It started with after-work drinks to blow off steam, and gathered speed the more often we drank together. Impaired by the alcohol and in despair over my broken business and strained marriage, I was desperate to feel alive and worthy again. I let go of my morals, ignored the vows I'd made to Mika, and jumped into the relationship in the hopes it would give me the emotional salve I needed. It was the worst thing I could have done and only made things far more difficult. Not long after my daughter was born, the affair was exposed.

This was my rock bottom. I had never, ever imagined I could be someone who would do something so terrible. I had lost all sense of who I was, and was consumed by feelings of shame and depression. I felt like I was engulfed in darkness, but in a clear moment I saw a light. This light was my newborn daughter, Reese. Looking at her I saw two paths ahead. The first path was the same *I* was handed as a child: divorced parents and accompanying baggage. The second path was a life with my family together, and two parents fully committed to each other. Sitting in her nursery, tears running down my face, I cried out to God and devoted myself to the second path. I would do anything and everything possible to move past this and save my marriage, my family, and my own life.

In the aftermath, at a time when we should have been more deeply in love than ever before, my marriage hung by a thread. Mika and I fought constantly, both overwhelmed by the betrayal and the hurricane of emotion and blame it had stirred up. I've never experienced anything so painful and frightening, and I know that had it not been for our newborn child, Mika and I would not have recovered. As much anguish as we were both suffering, Reese was an endless source of love and serenity, and we were determined to protect her from the situation raging outside her bedroom door. She doesn't know it yet, but that tiny girl held our family together through the worst year of our lives, and she was only a few weeks old.

Drinking is the status quo social activity in America. We have a few drinks here, a few drinks there, and make believe it's no big deal. And yet America is suffering from endemic problems that ruin thousands of lives every year, and alcohol is complicit in all of them. Divorce, obesity, and unemployment plague the nation. We joke about #dadbods and hangovers, but the situation serious — drinking puts our health at risk in ways we would never accept from any other pastime. Alcohol is directly linked to cancer, heart disease, and mental illness, and yet we guzzle it down like it's the elixir of life.

For some of us, drinking becomes a way to escape. It's our sedative of choice, allowing us to distance ourselves from the stress of the daily grind, from the dissatisfaction of our relationships and the nagging sense that life isn't turning out the way we had dreamed. I speak from experience — at the worst point of my drinking, I was sedating myself nightly to suppress the stress of my insanely dysfunctional business and to avoid thinking about the growing chasm in my marriage.

For many of us, a couple of drinks every few days is the norm and we can stop there. But once in awhile, perhaps in Vegas or on a night out with friends, one drink turns into ten and the next thing you know, it's Tuesday, you can't find your phone, and you're promising yourself for the twentieth time that you're never drinking again.

Other people never stop at one or two, no matter what day of the week it is. Every time turns into a bender, and as the weeks and years go by, drinking starts to account for an alarming portion of their lives.

No matter where you fall on the drinking spectrum, let's get one thing clear: Many of the negative decisions, actions, and outcomes in our lives happen because of alcohol. Whether the consequence is something "small," like having a subpar work day when you needed to be productive, or something "big," like getting slapped with a DUI and having your license revoked, drinking causes a *lot* of problems.

In my own family, the majority of men (both alive and deceased) have had major struggles, losses, and even deaths where alcohol played a role. In 2012, I reread a genealogy of our family my grandmother wrote before she passed away. Her story smacked me right between the eyes. Grandma Lou was explicit in describing the arrests, injuries, humiliations, and deaths suffered by the men in her life as a result of their drinking habits. Her account gave me a high-definition preview of my own future, and it scared the hell out of me. I no longer had an interest in drinking at a very deep level. My grandchildren would have a different story to read about their heritage.

The day Mika agreed to work on our marriage instead of ending it, I knew I had a hell of a road ahead of me. I had been drinking since I was about 15, and it permeated every part of my life. I didn't know who I was without alcohol, and so even then, I avoided drawing a line in the sand. All the damage I had done was directly linked to alcohol, but I couldn't bring myself to quit. Fortunately, I took the first step towards sobriety — cutting down my intake and honing in on what *really* mattered to me, slowly rebuilding the rest of my life around those priorities. I realized that if I really loved my wife and family, I had to start making real changes, and the first step to getting every part of my life back on track was getting completely honest and vulnerable with Mika.

At this point, the only thing we could really agree on was that we would do whatever it took to repair our marriage. We were completely isolated from each other, but we remembered how good our relationship had been in the past. We both knew we could have that joy and love again, but we didn't know how to move past everything that had happened. Without guidance, we would never be able to find our way, so we started going to Christian counseling with a fantastic therapist named Jamie Kobsar. One of the first things he told us shaped everything we've experienced since:

> *"You will not be able to have a loving, growth-oriented, long-term relationship if you don't have a solid foundation as individuals, and if you aren't coming into this relationship whole."*

That was extremely powerful. I had to take complete responsibility for myself, my behavior, and my reactions. Mika wasn't blameless either, and had to take complete responsibility for herself, for her behavior, and her reactions, but I had to accept that underneath it all, it was *my* choices that had led us to that point. We both had to acknowledge that neither of us were perfect, and had shortcomings far beyond what we had admitted to ourselves. We had both been selfish and shortsighted and we needed to invest in our relationship in a focused, radically honest way. Counselling also reminded us that neither of us had been to church in a very long time, except for the token Christmas services. Our deeper purpose and connection to God was non-existent, and we were living in a bubble of consumerism and self-sedation.

We agreed that we would start taking the family back to church, hoping it would create a sense of purpose for the family so we could get back to some semblance of normality. On our first day back at church, Mika and I were barely on speaking terms. She took the girls to the morning service, and I went to the service in the evening. Let's just say the 5 p.m. service did not have the bubbly, "kumbaya" vibe the morning services exuded! The pastor didn't even preach — the service was pre-recorded for the handful of people scattered around the room, many of whom were alone and hurting just like me.

Despite the digital delivery, the sermon I heard that night at Cornerstone Church in Chandler, Arizona, changed my life. In the middle of the biggest crisis I had ever faced, Pastor Linn Winters' sermon was about changing your family tree. The message came in loud and clear — each and every one of us has an opportunity to create a new branch of our family tree, to turn over a new leaf and trigger a change that will be revered and cherished by future generations, no matter how bleak our heritage might be.

The message hit me so hard that I sat crying in the back of the room long after the service had ended. As I began to calm down, a sense of purpose came over me like I had never experienced before. In that moment, I saw I had a chance to change my family tree, to free our family from substance abuse and heartache. I grew up in a broken home, as did my father, as did his father. God was speaking to me so clearly that day: we were done with that cycle. No more divorce, no more alcoholism, no more self-inflicted disasters.

I quit drinking soon after that service. I knew there was no way to change my family tree, to level up with Mika and to start a powerful new chapter in my life while alcohol was still on the table, so I let it go. No fuss, no big ceremony — on October 22nd, 2013, I didn't drink anything, and never have again.

In the months that followed that decision, I had plenty of opportunity to reflect on alcohol and the role it had played in my life. Over time, several questions crystallized, and soon it was bugging me enough that I knew it was time to write this book: why do we use a substance that so severely compromises our brain, which is the only tool we have to get ahead in life? Why do we sacrifice our focus, priorities and energy to something that drains us? Why can't we think objectively about the impact alcohol really has on us?

The only answer I can find is that we are conditioned to think it's normal to drink. Drinking is heavily advertised as a symbol of celebration, and it's an ingrained part of our culture. We drink on birthdays and anniversaries, holidays and sports events, at graduations and when we close business deals. It's an easy way for us to create bonding experiences with other people (even if those experiences actually end up being shallow as a result of the alcohol).

It was this social element I was most afraid of losing when I decided to quit drinking. I thought date nights with Mika would awkward or tense if I abstained, or that my friends would suddenly think I was boring. As it turned out, *no one cared*. From my wife and friends, to my work colleagues, family and church members — no one even blinked. Now, after several years of being sober, I know what life can be like when you're operating at full capacity every day. It's pretty amazing, and so in this book we're going to talk about kicking ass in every part of life, no matter where you're starting from right now.

My life today is unrecognizable from what it was the day I quit, and your life can go the same way. Every part of my life — my health, my marriage, my business — has experienced a major upgrade, and in addition to sobriety, I've included a lot of the personal systems, habits, and tools I've used to optimize my life that can have a powerful impact for you too.

These are the systems I've used to create massive success in my business, Design Pickle, while building a thriving, healthy family. I'm a normal guy, just like you. I am not famous and don't have any special advantages over anyone else. I grew up in Tucson, Arizona, and now call Scottsdale, AZ, my home base. My mom lives close by, and my sister isn't far away either. My wife is a stay-at-home mom, and we have three girls who go to local schools. While we now enjoy a high quality of life, the system behind *The Sober Entrepreneur* came into being in very "normal" circumstances, which means that no matter what your situation is, you'll be able to use it yourself. You don't need any special talents or connections, you don't need any edge-case hacks. All you need to do is read, and if the words hit you where it hurts, start applying them to your own life as soon as you can.

Before we take the plunge, hear this: Sobriety gives, and drinking (or any kind of self-medication) takes away. When I was a drinker, my life was continually drained. There was a hole in every bucket — time, energy, money, health, and relationships — and I was in a constant state of scarcity and fear, trying to plug the holes and replace the losses. I didn't realize I was punching new holes and spilling any gains down the sink every time I picked up a drink. Now that I'm sober, my life is continually filled. Those buckets are overflowing — I have far more time, energy, and money to spend on whatever I want. My relationships and health are more solid and vibrant, and my life is the definition of abundance. I'm eager and excited every morning to discover what lies ahead, and that can be your life, too, if you're ready to make it happen.

CHAPTER TWO: WE ALL HAVE PROBLEMS

Our culture is increasingly obsessed with the myth of the entrepreneur. Men like Steve Jobs, Elon Musk, Jeff Bezos, and Mark Zuckerberg are held up as paragons of achievement — the pinnacle of success as our world defines it. While we're all starstruck by how much money they've made, we're also obsessed with their *work*, their *hustle*, and their obsession with their craft. Many of the entrepreneurs we celebrate are known for working obscene hours, destroying their health, and burning their personal relationships to the ground in the name of their business and driving vision.

This fixation seeps into our psyches. We begin to associate more work with better results. For years I firmly believed that the answer to my money problems was to simply work harder and longer, instead of choosing better projects to work on, or looking for opportunities with higher leverage. Whether we realize it or not, we're constantly encouraged to work more — to hustle, grind, sleep when we're dead — in order to be successful. But this approach just doesn't work. For most people, working 100-hour weeks or sleeping three or four hours a night is more likely to result in hospitalization or divorce than a huge, profitable business or a multi-million dollar exit.

This is what's known as survivor bias: only the people who survive the entrepreneurial gauntlet can tell the story. You don't hear about the people who don't make it, and this is compounded by the social media "highlight reel." When we look at successful entrepreneurs, we see only the wins. Even with all the "transparency" online these days, no one *really* puts their failures out for the public to scrutinize in real time. That's the privilege of success — you can share the near-misses when you're out of the danger zone and can afford to look back and laugh. But when failure is looming, or we're still in the danger zone, we don't want to tell *anyone*. There's a fear, buried away, that somehow talking about it would be the final straw, that publicizing the struggle would destroy people's confidence in us, we'd be seen as a failure, a liar, a fool. We decide that the only way out is to power forward, head down and alone.

Social media drives the highlight reel fallacy to outrageous heights. Entire brands are built on fake images and "product partnerships." Behind the scenes, Facebook and Google are laughing all the way to the bank, with a whole generation of consumers now addicted to this content. In our personal lives, social media creates a false "social contract" we feel compelled to adhere to with the people in our lives. It's like we've all agreed that we will only share the good stuff. If we don't have something good to say, then we won't say anything at all… even if saying what's really happening could change everything for the better. Instead of being real with people (both online and in person), we let our internal dialogue scare us into silence: *"No one wants to hear about this. I should be able to handle it myself. This is no one's problem. I brought this on myself. I don't want people to know about what's really going on."*

When I was in the depth of my addiction and affair, no one knew. Not a single person. There was no one I felt I could talk to, no one that understood the trouble I was in, no one that even knew I was struggling. I'd been playing the highlight reel game for so long that I didn't know how to bridge that gap, even with Mika or my best friends, and this situation plays out over and over again in our country. According to the American

Psychological Association, nearly one in 10 men in the US have an ongoing, daily battle with depression and isolation.[1] American men are four times more likely than women to commit suicide, and the rates get worse as we get older.

This is why addiction in America is so rampant. Studies from the National Institute on Drug Abuse show that men are also more likely to use all kinds of drugs than women, have higher rates of dependence on those drugs, and are more likely to end up in the emergency room or worse.[2] Almost 80% of the people suffering with substance abuse struggle with alcohol, and one in eight of us are using other drugs along with the booze. The men of this country feel alone, and we're trying to fix it by self-medicating.

But most guys will tell you they don't have a problem. Maybe you're reading this, thinking, "Look, Russ, this is a good story, but I don't have this kind of problem. I'm not an addict." And you might be right… you might not be an addict, but you do have a problem. We all have a problem. Yours might be the obsession with your work, the marijuana, painkillers, or Adderall, but you wouldn't be reading this book if everything in your life was peachy.

In case you still think you're the exception, let's go over a few of the common ways people rationalize sedation. I reference drinking here, but feel free to replace it with your habit of choice:

- *Drinking takes the edge off. I'm just using it to relax.*

Drinking takes nothing away; it just suppresses and delays whatever you're dealing with. Why do you need a chemical intervention to be able to unwind from your business? What is the true root of your stress? Is it your product, your process, your people? What would it take to resolve that stress instead of hiding from it?

- *I only drink socially. If I was drinking alone I might think there was a problem.*

This is a logical fallacy — those two points are actually disconnected. Drinking socially has nothing to do with how much you drink. Drinking alone *can* be problematic, but it would be better to have one drink alone than eight with a friend. Drinking socially makes it acceptable to go overboard and relinquish your self-control to "group think" as the night goes on. Drinking also makes you worse in social situations, so even if you do only drink socially, you're doing yourself a double disservice: you think more of yourself and less of others.

You are less perceptive and more likely to say or do something that's out of line. Not to mention that you remember and experience less as the world becomes dull around you.

- *I have more fun when I drink! I can be a b it uncomfortable around other people.*

It's easy to forget that alcohol is a depressant. Let me spell this out: Drinking makes you psychologically depressed.[3] The boost in excitement and energy is short lived — you get a buzz from the first few drinks, and then you start to slump. The uptick of fun from a few drinks is temporary, and always makes you feel flat the next day. You might not feel sad or sick or unable to get out of bed, but at the least you'll feel unmotivated and irritable. These are the symptoms of your nervous system, hormones, and neurochemicals dealing with all the depressant chemicals in the alcohol you drank the night before.

- *I never get out of control with drinking.*

Not everyone gets so drunk that they get kicked out of bars all the time. The worst effects of the drinking lifestyle are gradually, quietly destructive — it's never about that one crazy night that goes wrong.

Your relationships become strained when you drink because you make promises you don't keep, you say things you don't mean, and you're not fully present when people need you to be. Your body and health degrade, you make worse food choices when you drink, and you skip workouts when you're hungover. At work, you make mistakes because you're functioning below your ability, and you don't have the focus to respond effectively to what's happening around you. As all these things compound over time, your sense of self-worth slowly degrades. Drinking chips away at you over years and decades, and often you only notice how far you've fallen because something finally goes sideways.

- *A drink or two helps me get to sleep. Otherwise my brain is whirring all night.*

I'm sorry to tell you, but this one is a total myth. Being a depressant, alcohol *does* make you feel tired. You might fall asleep faster, but the quality of your sleep is so negatively impacted that you might as well stay awake. A good night's sleep isn't about how fast you fall asleep; it's the result of how much deep sleep (known as REM sleep) you get through the night. Studies have found that using alcohol to fall asleep *reduces* the amount of deep sleep you get later in the night.[4] It would be more effective to spend a few minutes before bed writing down everything that comes into your head so that everything is processed and your brain can unwind without any anxiety about forgetting important information.

- *I'm not an entrepreneur...*

Most of the people reading this book are entrepreneurs already, but if you haven't made the leap yet, these concepts still apply to you. You don't have to have a business to understand that when you're responsible for generating your own income (and that of any employees), it's critical to show up sharp and on your A-game every day.

If you don't want to be an entrepreneur, that's perfectly fine, but don't show up and half-ass at your job. Commit. Do the hard things. Be the best damn employee your company has ever had. Your life will be infinitely richer if you give your best effort in everything you do — and getting rid of alcohol will help you on that path.

For some people, the choice to remain employed has been a crutch that *allows you to keep drinking*. You can hide in the corporate grind without too much accountability. Hear me now: The long-term path to freedom is in *your* hands, not in the hands of an executive team. If you ever want to head out into the entrepreneurial unknown, I can promise you that doing it sober will give you a massive advantage.

DO THE MATH

At the time of writing this book, I have not woken up tired from a hangover in over three years. As you might imagine, my productivity has gone through the roof. How much more productive would you have been — mathematically, on paper — if you hadn't been drinking for the past year? Two years? Five? Ten?

Let's say you have five hungover hours per week — two nights out with two to three hours of reduced productivity the next day, which is a pretty normal schedule for most people. They might not be horrible hangovers, but your mind isn't as sharp as it could be and your body is definitely not performing at its peak. That's 260 hours hungover per year (and that's not increasing the number to account for holidays and big events that write off the whole next day). That's nearly 11 days per year that go to being hungover and *not* working on your business, or being present with your family, or improving yourself.

People don't realize this about drinking. They wonder why they're not losing weight, why their business isn't growing like they want, or why their relationships feel shallow or disconnected. For many of us, drinking is the obstacle. It's nearly invisible, but it's the one thing standing between us and everything we want most.

The problem, of course, is that most of us don't feel like addicts.

Disclaimer: This calculation is not meant to be a downer. I am not recommending you become a hermit who never leaves your house and works all day and all night. While that is one path to sobriety, it's not a fun one. You can keep an active social life — just know there's an entirely new experience waiting to unfold!

Since I am a total nerd, I developed the following timetable to calculate the real hour cost of drinking. Using a highly sophisticated predictive model, we can use three very scientific terms to categorize each drinking occasion:

- *Solo Time: A couple of drinks at the end of the day to take the edge off*

- *Social Time: A low-key event like a date or dinner out with friends*
- *Party Time: A blowout, lose-your-phone-wake-up-in-a-park kind of night*

Using the same scientific method, we can break out each event into three blocks of time:

- *Before: Time spent before the event. Travel time, coordinating plans, and so on*
- *During: Time spent at the actual event (and perhaps additional unplanned time because the event is unexpectedly awesome)*
- *After: Recovery time after your drinking escapades*

	Solo Time	Social Time	Party Time
Before	30 minutes	1 hour	2 hours
During	2 hours	3 hours	5 hours
After*	2 hours	4 hours	12 hours
Total	4.5 hours	8 hours	19 hours

* Note: 'After' time increases with age. These times are based off of my average, 30-year old body (the last data point I have from drinking).

Obviously, this "scientific" method is really a set of very rough averages, but do the math for yourself. An average night out drinking can eat up eight hours — enough time for a full day of work. My nights out took up far more time than these averages, and maybe yours do too. The drinking and recovery time can take up an entire 24-hour day, or more.

Losing that much time occasionally is one thing, but when you work out how much time is squandered over months and years of regular drinking, it's a slap in the face. Just one social event a week (at home or with friends) could mean months or years of time dedicated to drinking. Even with modest calculations, you could feasibly attribute at least 5,000 hours over a 10-year drinking career to drinking. Imagine what your business, relationships or personal abilities would look like if you had used those 5,000 hours differently in the last 10 years!

Occasionally, we might think there's a problem. Let's say you go out and wake up regretting the tequila shots and beer rounds. You think to yourself, *"I am never drinking again. For real this time. I am so done with this. I'm going to see what's online about quitting drinking."*

Unfortunately, there's no middle ground in the literature. All the material about drinking problems is specifically directed at addicts or people whose lives are totally destroyed from their substance issues. You are either a full-blown addict, or you don't have an issue at all. There is no conversation around this topic for people who haven't hit rock bottom yet, even though we'd all agree it's much better to turn things around before you do bottom out.

When I went to my first AA meeting, I suddenly felt like I was overreacting. Several people there were in very extreme situations, some of them barely hanging on, and while it gave me a clear perspective on what would happen to me if I kept drinking, I felt like an outsider. Feeling so disconnected from the dire experiences of the rest of the group, I realized it would be hard for me to maintain my commitment to sobriety if I relied on that particular group for support. Things in my life weren't *that* bad, and I knew I would be able to rationalize my behavior if I measured it against their situations, so I kept looking for a good solution that was closer to my experience.

It took a while, but eventually I found a group of people who had similar values and situations to me in the Celebrate Recovery program at a local church. I cannot emphasize how important it is to be able to talk with people you have a shared experience with, because you feel more comfortable being your authentic self. You don't have to censor how you talk about things to contextualize or soften them for other people; everyone already understands where you are coming from. I still support and participate in Celebrate Recovery, and I even helped launch a chapter at Impact Church in Scottsdale, but I still see a gap in the resources that are out there for people who are simply thinking about quitting.

And here's the thing: if you're an entrepreneur, functioning below your ability is living life on hard mode. When your progress and results are directly related to how much energy and focus you can put into something, drinking is just shooting yourself in the foot. You are voluntarily handicapping yourself, turning hard into hellacious.

So if you're trying to build something big, new, or life changing, I want to throw you a challenge: which is more important to you? The business or the booze? If you could choose only one, which would it be?

If your answer is the business, you're already on the right path.

FINDING YOUR *WHY*

There are plenty of ways you can quit, and I've tried most of them. There's everything from gradually reducing your consumption, to support groups like AA or Celebrate Recovery, to accountability partnerships, books, blogs, and professional counseling.

These external support systems will certainly have a significant, positive impact on your situation. However, if your change is externally driven — by other people, systems, or programs — you will eventually find a way to justify drinking again.

Perhaps it's a birthday, date night, vacation, wedding, or just one hell of a day dealing with a terrible client. One drink eventually turns into three. Maybe that day, maybe later on after the door has been opened again, those three drinks explode into a 16-hour-tailgate-party-bus-extravaganza, followed by the hangover to end all hangovers, and you're back to square one.

Quitting drinking doesn't start with a program or a system. It starts with the answer to one question:

Why?

Why should you quit?

If you're not sure, rephrase the question: What is more important in your life than drinking? What legacy do you want to leave? If you still don't have an answer, something deep and real, don't give up on the thought exercise. I couldn't answer this question for many years. I tried to quit drinking about a dozen times before it stuck, because every time, my motivation came from external sources. It came from other people, or from my desire to do something for other people: I wanted to lose weight so I would be more attractive; I made a mistake and wanted to make amends with Mika I needed to clean up my act at work. I was always trying to quit for something external.

My *why* landed in my lap after many years of searching. My *why* was to change my family tree. To leave a legacy for my kids, and their kids, that was positive, influential, and godly. I wanted to stop the cycle of isolation, addiction, and pain that had tortured my family for generations. To do that would require an entirely new version of Russ Perry — someone I couldn't even imagine at the time. But one thing was for sure. I wouldn't be able to do it with alcohol keeping me weak and distracted.

Don't get me wrong — external motivation will have an impact on your sobriety. But you are battling a deep-rooted habit that has been etched into your routine and biochemistry for years or even decades. External motivation is just not enough. Anything external fades over time, because we forget, and priorities change. People forgive and forget, and soon we go back to the same old circumstances, letting ourselves get stuck in a self-defeating loop. We go back to the same old patterns, we lose a little more of ourselves, and the next time things get just a little bit worse.

It's just like chopping down a tree. With enough time on the receiving end of an axe, even the strongest trees can fall.

Finding your true *why* — something rooted so deep in you that it transcends any social conviction — is the only permanent path to sobriety. It's the only thing that will make that axe bounce off you without leaving a mark.

You find your courage and conviction to quit when you stand alone, when you are prepared to be your own motivation, without relying on pressure from anyone else. I found my *why* that night in the evening service at Cornerstone Church. Sobriety alone wouldn't change my family tree, but it would become a central part of the foundation that is now enabling me to build greatness into all areas of my life.

To overcome alcohol (or any other substance you might struggle with), it's critical to find your *why* and a greater sense of purpose within yourself. These will be constant sources of focus, resilience and strength over the course of your life. Your *why* will make you strong when you feel weak, comfort you when you are scared or doubting, and bring you a deeper sense of joy and fulfillment than you believe is possible right now.

YOUR BUSINESS IS NOT YOUR *WHY*

Love, marriage, and children are incredibly powerful motivations to live a better life, but even men with extraordinary families still lose their way. There has to be something deeper at work, an internal sense of purpose that transcends everything else, and one of the most common mistakes entrepreneurial men make is to believe that business will give you that deeper purpose, and that creating financial success is the only key to a prosperous and fulfilling life.

It's not hard to follow the logic: We have the responsibility to provide for our family, take care of our kids, create a better life than our parents had, and have some fun along the way. The cultural obsession with entrepreneurship makes it seem like creating a business is the ultimate way to build a fulfilling and free life.

If you've been in the game for a while, you know two things about this: business *can* be fulfilling, and creating your own resources *can* lead to freedom. It can also become a nightmarish prison of your own making. Entrepreneurship is not for the faint of heart.

Nearly every entrepreneur I know has been through some brutal stuff to make their business work. Most of us have scars and wounds that stay with us, sometimes for life. Many of us sacrifice our health, others sacrifice their relationships, and we all suffer intense anxiety, stress, frustration, and fear (often for *years*) before we make something work. And we are willing to go through it all because we truly believe life will be better on the other side.

Here are a few of the guiding beliefs or "scripts" most entrepreneurs start out with. Some of them sound ridiculous when they're written down on paper, but most of us seem to have beliefs like this running somewhere in our subconscious minds:

- To have the life I want, I first must succeed professionally.
- Building a successful business will make me feel loved and worthy as a human.
- My bank account is a reflection of my success.
- I cannot allow failure or admit defeat, no matter the cost or the evidence that I should move on.
- Success will come if I just work harder.
- The only people that deserve happiness, rest, and fulfillment are the people who have built a successful business.

The stories and scripts that run our lives are incredibly powerful. They shape our actions, attitudes, and priorities, and we often aren't even aware of them. They accumulate in our brains over time from our family, friends, and culture. They are often so ingrained that we float along believing it all, never questioning whether these scripts are actually true.

This is critical to understand, because the belief that success begets happiness is false. A business is not your *why*. A business is not the key to unlocking what we want from life. That comes from within ourselves.

Can your business be aligned with your personal values? Absolutely. Can your business enable you to achieve purpose-driven outcomes? Of course. But your business is not some magical extension of who you are or an expression of your worth as a human. The *only* purpose of any business, especially one you create, is to generate wealth. Period. It's not there to help you define yourself, to enhance your relationships, or to heal a wound in your life. It's there to create value on both sides of a transaction — the value of what's delivered to your customers, and the value of the money you are paid to deliver it.

Now, wealth matters. But wealth is a means to an end, not an end in itself. Like building a business, building wealth is not a purpose. Building wealth will not bring you happiness, or life balance, or good relationships with your family. Building wealth puts dollars in the bank. You can use it to fund a purposeful life, and to provide a great environment for your family. But you cannot use it to create meaning for yourself. For this reason, our *why* must be clear before we pursue wealth. Having a clear *why* allows us to use and control our wealth as a tool, rather than being ruled by it.

Our *why* is a beacon we can follow through life.

We can measure every decision against our *why*. If a decision will take you away from your *why*, you know it's not the right choice. If a decision will help you achieve your *why*, then you know you're on the right path. Having wealth helps you to achieve everything you want to do, but your real success in life will come from knowing what really gives you meaning and fulfillment.

---

[1] http://www.apa.org/monitor/2015/12/numbers.aspx

[2] https://www.drugabuse.gov/publications/research-reports/substance-use-in-women/sex-gender-differences-in-substance-use

[3] https://www.drinkaware.co.uk/alcohol-facts/health-effects-of-alcohol/mental-health/alcohol-and-mental-health/

[4] https://www.drinkaware.co.uk/alcohol-facts/health-effects-of-alcohol/effects-on-the-body/alcohol-and-sleep/

CHAPTER THREE: SEDATION IS THE ENEMY

Entrepreneurs are often "Type A" people — goal-oriented, focused and internally motivated; and at the same time, prone to anxiety, high stress levels, and self-doubt. We're prime candidates for self-sedation.

To me it seems like some cosmic joke: *"Here's the most exciting, rewarding path you can take through life! Now, earn it by running this gauntlet of emotional torture."*

We all know entrepreneurs who think it's normal to get symptoms of anxiety every time they open their email or chat. Maybe you're one of them, and you feel that it's normal to go through every day second-guessing yourself, constantly on high alert for everything that could go wrong, and that it's normal to need a few stiff drinks at the end of the day to cope with the stress of it all. But while self-medication is common, it's not normal.

Self-medication (the technical term for using a substance to take the edge off) is defined as "the use of drugs to treat self-diagnosed disorders or symptoms." Sound familiar? If you've ever wondered whether you suffer from anxiety, depression, a rage disorder, or, on the flipside, a lack of empathy or real feeling of any kind, then using a substance to help you feel different might have seemed like a natural next step.

Research published in the Harvard Review of Psychiatry describes it like this:

> *"Individuals discover that the specific actions or effects of each class of drugs relieve or change a range of painful affect states. Self-medication factors occur in a context of self-regulation vulnerabilities—primarily difficulties in regulating affects, self-esteem, relationships, and self-care. Persons with substance use disorders suffer in the extreme with their feelings, either being overwhelmed with painful affects or seeming not to feel their emotions at all. Substances of abuse help such individuals to relieve painful affects or to experience or control emotions when they are absent or confusing."* [1]

Or, in words the rest of us can understand, we all prefer different substances to help us handle the painful emotions and experiences in our lives. We use our substance of choice when those feelings overwhelm us, when we feel terrible about ourselves or our businesses, when our relationships are in the dumps, or when we're not looking after ourselves properly. If you're someone who feels their emotions too intensely (or not intensely enough), your substance of choice will help you feel like you've got it under control.

Unfortunately, that's a false sense of security.

Having a few drinks or some Xanax to take the edge off at night also makes you dull the next day. Crushing Red Bulls, candy, or cocaine late into the day might get you through your to-do list, but you'll be buzzing long after you go to bed, you'll barely sleep, and so the next day the cycle has to start again.

Culturally, self-medication or sedation is an acceptable behaviour. We don't like dealing with difficult emotions, and it's much easier to smoke something than to do the work to resolve the actual problem. We medicate our kids when they're too energetic, and we medicate ourselves when we have too many feelings. We turn a blind eye when we see other people medicating their feelings away so as not to shame them, and to avoid having to look at our own behavior.

Sedation is not limited to alcohol. Drug use, casual sex, gambling, shopping, watching TV and eating junk food, and under- or over-eating can all be sedative behaviors. All these behaviors can start out innocently enough, but over time can become powerful, damaging forces in our lives. They are subtractive behaviors, as opposed to additive behaviors.

Subtractive behaviors often feel great on the front end. They tap into our biology to release endorphins (the feel-good chemicals in our brains), but they leave us high and dry after the initial buzz wears off. On the other hand, additive behaviors leave us with positive feelings, long after the behavior is finished. Some additive behaviors include working out, meditating, having sex with your partner, building something from raw materials, creating music or art, and travel.

Now, sometimes people tell me to lighten up. *"Come on, Russ. What's the big deal if people eat a Kit-Kat and have a joint every now and again?"* And I have to agree that occasional indulgences are *not* a big deal, and I have no interest in judging or condemning anyone's choices. But you have to be able to tell the difference between occasional indulgence and self-medication, because subtractive behaviors are engineered to be addictive, and none of us can outsmart the systems that sell those substances. Someone is always profiting from your participation, and your biology is always working against you.

Self-medication creates a sticky web that stops you from being at your best. And when you run your own business, that is an expense no one can afford.

When we self-medicate to try to *increase* our chances of success, we actually *reduce* our chances over the long run. Coming to work when we're not at our best is self-sabotage. A hangover (from alcohol, sugar, or just an accumulation of bad choices) will stop you from engaging fully with what's happening around you each day, but it also stops you from seeing opportunities and threats.

The relentless pursuit of success, with all the ups and downs, can also erode every other part of our lives, even without all the uppers and downers you could use along the way. Our health and relationships suffer the most. Even when it *feels* like there's not a problem, the emotional cycles of entrepreneurship can create extremely unhealthy patterns in how we treat our bodies and the people around us.

When things are going well, you get comfortable. You don't really notice if you start having a few more glasses of wine than you used to at meals, or if the occasional desserts are starting to stack up around your waist. You don't notice that you and your spouse are skipping date nights, or that your evenings are focused on Facebook at the expense of your family. Comfort breeds inertia.

Most entrepreneurs reading this book *aren't* at rock bottom. You probably have a decent life — a successful business, peaceful home life, and no big problems to speak of. Things are going well… but for a lot of us, that's almost more dangerous than actually having everything go down in flames. After a few years of these patterns you might wake up one day to find yourself hungover, 30 pounds overweight, and getting served with divorce papers.

I have seen people get divorced after four, five, 10 years in a relationship because they just don't know each other anymore. The sedation has seeped into their lives and dulled their connection to each other. There often weren't any big fights or blow-outs, but years of going out to drink with friends instead of going on date nights together led them down different paths. Getting the bigger house and the better car got prioritized over building the deeper relationship, and eventually they just became roommates with a lot of shared bills and responsibilities.

Don't let that become your story.

Simple changes can make a huge difference over a lifetime. *The Washington Post* interviewed couples who had been married 40 years or more, wanting to know the secret to a long and healthy relationship. At the top of the list? Connection, laughter, and, yes, date nights.[2] Go out on a date with your partner once a week instead of going out with your buddies every time. Even this small change in trajectory will have a massive compounding effect on your relationship capital, and 10 years from now you will be deeply connected to your partner instead of looking at a stranger across the room that you used to be married to.

Some people would argue that hitting rock bottom is the only way to wake up to a life of sedation. At least when your behavior sends you crashing down to the pits of despair, you can see that the only way out is up. It's easier to change in extreme circumstances than to change when you're comfortable and there's no acute pain to propel you forward.

Sedation is a siren song, but distracting ourselves from the intensity and uncertainty of our lives leads only to lives half-lived. Whether it's alcohol, food, weed, cigarettes, caffeine, painkillers, or some other substance or behavior you lean on for relief, the effect of consumption increases exponentially over the years. Research published in the scientific journal *Addiction* draws a direct, causative line from drinking alcohol to higher rates of diagnosis for seven of the most common cancers.[3] Many relationships fracture and fall apart as the alcohol-fueled behavior takes its toll. These seemingly innocent habits — a few drinks here and there, watching the game to avoid the conversation — compound over time and can crush the most important parts of your life.

Let me be clear here. Some people can create amazing things and achieve real greatness without going sober. Many successful people still drink. There are NFL players, professional musicians, and business owners who have changed the game in their field and done it while having a few drinks every now and then. It's not impossible to be successful in your professional and personal life without being sober — it's just *harder*. If you have an addictive personality, it's also more dangerous. Entrepreneurship is hard enough already, so why stack the deck against yourself? Even if you don't care a single bit about building a family or getting fit and you just want crazy amounts of cash, sobriety tips the odds your way.

The way I see it, God gave me the standard-issue body and mind. My mom was a single parent who worked as a teacher without any wealth or family money to rely on. The hand I was dealt in life was not exactly stacked in my favor. That means it's up to me to take every advantage I can get my hands on. Sobriety has a real strategic element: if it's me, sober, versus the standard-issue guy who still drinks, I'm going to be up earlier, thinking clearly and firing on all cylinders. While the other guy is still feeling flat and dusty in the afternoon, I'm going to be in the gym feeling great, building more energy to keep working to the end of the day, making better decisions, and constantly moving forward towards my next goal. I will win, every time.

BRING YOUR RUTHLESS COMMITMENT

One of the most influential training programs I have ever participated in is Wake Up Warrior, founded by Garrett J. White. A core message of the program is that any man can accomplish massive success in all areas of his life if he commits to it. Garrett teaches that the only thing men have to do is show up, do the work, and maintain a ruthless commitment to achieving their desired results. We'll talk more about Warrior later in the book, but if you are ready to let go of the sedation you've been chasing in your own life, then it's time to find that commitment within yourself.

Showing up with ruthless commitment means honoring your commitment to yourself and your family to do the work required to achieve your goals, no matter how hard, tiring, or frustrating things become. How many times have you put in less than 100% of your effort? How many times have you rationalized sleeping in, or put off a hard decision until you "feel better"? If you're still drinking, I bet the frequency is higher than you'd like to admit. When we are ruthlessly committed, those failures fall away and we'll do whatever it takes to make progress. The new path ahead matters more than the old habits behind.

To achieve the life you want, we've already discussed that a clear *why* must be your foundation. The next step is to have a few specific, concrete targets to focus on over the long term. When I started Warrior, my *why* was (and is still) to change my family tree. This is big, moving, and grandiose. My targets were simple:

- Spend the next summer in California with my family
- Train for and compete in a local Crossfit competition
- Grow my business to over $80,000 in monthly recurring revenue

Coupled with the dramatic change in my behavior after quitting alcohol, these outcomes were realistic and attainable. They gave me a deeper motivation to stay sober too — I was passionately dedicated to achieving each of those targets, which created huge motivation for me to stay away from alcohol. As you think about what your own targets might be, choose things that matter to you personally, and keep it simple. Your targets need to be important enough that you feel inspired and motivated to achieve them, but they should not be so enormous that they cause you anxiety or are unrealistic to achieve in the next few months.

Want to learn more about setting targets and my recommended books on the topic? Go to soberentrepreneur.com/bonus

---

Sobriety gave me an edge I had not been able to get any other way. It helped me get out of my head, build a deeper connection with my wife, create a business that has crushed its competitors, and develop an entire niche in the creative services market. At its core, Design Pickle is a graphic design company that faces immense competition from local designers, marketplaces, and even AI-based tools… yet we've doubled in size every year since launch and are on our way to becoming an eight-figure business.

All of this was only possible after the fog of drinking had lifted. The new clarity meant I was able to find my deeper *why* and a ruthless commitment to achieving the targets throughout every area of my life. Design Pickle would not exist today had I kept drinking. I might have had the idea, and might have even tried to start the business, but there is no way I would have succeeded at the level we are currently experiencing. Life is a game, and if you're playing to win, you've got to take every advantage.

---

[1] https://www.ncbi.nlm.nih.gov/pubmed/9385000

[2] https://www.washingtonpost.com/lifestyle/magazine/the-secret-to-a-long-lasting-marriage/2016/02/09/7faefe02-aff8-11e5-9ab0-884d1cc4b33e_story.html

[3] https://www.theguardian.com/society/2016/jul/22/alcohol-direct-cause-seven-forms-of-cancer-study

CHAPTER FOUR ADDICTED TO THE HUSTLE

Our conversation around addiction in this book has focused so far on alcohol and other physical substances. A large group of men would never consider themselves addicted to anything — they have a good professional track record, their drinking is a non-issue, and their marriage and kids are doing just fine.

But when you take a closer look at their business, it's a different story. They are compelled to work constantly — always checking email, responding to chats, taking unscheduled calls, and justifying it all as being necessary to the business. Of course, all those things could wait, and the behavior is just another way of soothing anxiety.

Or maybe things *are* on the brink of disaster, and the business is a step away from rock bottom as a result of their dysfunctional behavior. Maybe you've experienced a few of these symptoms in your own business:

- *You don't pay yourself consistently or at a market rate, and your personal finances struggle as a result*
- *You pay yourself above market rates or distribute profits too aggressively and find the business accounts empty when you have expenses to pay*
- *Your team is perpetually in crisis mode, either putting out fires with clients, starting fires with clients, or warring amongst themselves*
- *You have no time for your family, and your friends don't even try to see you anymore*
- *Your client relationships are all personal and you feel like all of them require your personal attention*
- *You feel obligated to be physically "at work" (or in your email or chat) as much as possible*
- *If the business does grow, your expenses and headaches increase proportionally because you don't have the systems in place to handle the new workload*
- *You are deathly afraid of losing a few key employees because no one else knows how to do what they do*

- *You do not believe that anyone else could understand or lead your business effectively*
- *You believe working more is the primary path to improving your success and quality of life*

This list sounds like madness. On paper, it seems crazy to allow even one of these elements into your business. But over the years I've seen men wake up day after day, year after year, sometimes for decades, to deal with these exact situations.

Why do they persist? Why can't they see how much damage they're doing to themselves and the business? Why don't they change, just cut their losses, or start again?

There are two major reasons entrepreneurs tolerate internal dysfunction: sunk-cost fallacy, and an addiction to the highs and lows of business just like any other chemical addiction. The sunk-cost fallacy happens when we convince ourselves that we've spent too many of our resources to turn back now. The addiction happens when our neurochemistry gets knotted up with the roller coaster ride of a dysfunctional business: we have an intense adrenalin surge in response to each crisis, then we get a hit of feel-good chemicals like dopamine and serotonin when we find the solution. It's just like taking a drug, and this one-two punch leaves us acting similar to people who stay in abusive relationships: they can see that things are bad, and that this isn't how it should be, but they can't see a different way to do things. They feel like there's too much to lose, and they're scared of what will happen if they walk away.

Addiction isn't rational, and once the high wears off, it's not fun either. Addiction happens when we burn ourselves a neural pathway that demands regular surges of feel-good chemicals to the brain.[1] Those of us addicted to dysfunctional businesses are no different, and the high of solving big conflicts and putting out fires feeds that neurological need. Entrepreneurs find a way to design their environments to support the things that make them feel good in that business context, and often that means allowing disasters to keep happening.

There are lots of ways the entrepreneur can experience this:

- Needing to be involved in every part of the business, no matter how menial
- Micromanaging staff and projects
- Creating recurring crises that can only be saved by the entrepreneur
- Understaffing the business or repeatedly making bad hires

- Expecting junior staff to succeed at senior level responsibilities
- Taking risks (through purchases, expansion, or acquisitions) that the business can't absorb

For many men, the real addiction at the core of these behaviors is being the hero. Each behavior thrusts the business into chaos, and the entrepreneur gets validation after validation by saving themselves and their company from the constant flow of crises. They subconsciously hardwire their business to be fundamentally flawed, so they can maintain their position as the hero. Without even realizing it, they develop a savior complex — they're constantly needed, and it makes them feel valuable and worthy.

I know because I was that guy!

During the eight years running my creative agencies, we found ourselves in crisis mode more times than I could possibly count… and I got to save the day every time.

When a big account decided they were going to walk, I would salvage the relationship. When a once-in-a-lifetime deal was on the line, I'd stay up all night to make it happen. When a key employee had a meltdown over the workload, I'd step in and make up the difference. When we couldn't find enough cash to make payroll, I'd sacrifice my own pay to ensure the checks cleared.

Russ Perry was a hero! I got the praise and recognition for saving the business every time… even if I was the one who put it at risk in the first place.

As with any addiction, the brain eventually develops a resistance to these behaviors. Soon enough, the validation that initially triggered the hero's high isn't enough anymore. The entrepreneur who is addicted to a chaotic business starts taking bigger risks, both professionally and personally. Eventually these risks create such serious problems that the business is faced with an existential threat. And if the business is not providing the business owner with enough opportunities to be the hero, the owner either...

- *Abandons the business and starts a new one to save*
- *Damage his personal life (often introducing drugs, extravagant spending, pornography, or alcohol), to create situations that need a savior*
- *Goes completely supernova, burning down his business and destroying his personal life in one hit, achieving full martyrdom*

As someone who has experienced both an addiction to

alcohol and to playing the savior, I've seen first-hand how entrepreneurship can be a very real gateway to addiction. Not only can we become addicted to the crisis-resolution cycles of a dysfunctional business, but we are at greater risk of bringing addictive substances into our lives to help us cope with the stress of it all. I firmly believe that we need to have more conversations around this topic to help men and their families balance their personal lives and their work.

Once I had made it through the journey towards balance, I was determined to do things differently with my most recent (and most successful) project, Design Pickle. Sobriety aside, I set out to build an organization that was not codependent on my emotional state. Because of the clarity I had developed before opening our virtual doors, I never allowed myself to become addicted to our success or failure.

———

Western society measures a man by how many zeros show up on his bank statement. The more money an entrepreneur makes, the more successful we consider him,. Mainstream media doesn't seem to care if he is healthy or present with his family or contributes to his community; we only care about the revenue he generates, the next big valuation, and the profit he takes home. In every industry (not just entrepreneurship), men are expected to make more at almost any cost. Children are expected to put up with an absent father in exchange for a big house and good school. Our wives are expected to be grateful for the lifestyle, even if it costs them their happiness and their connection with the person they love most in the world.

But a great lifestyle and true happiness do not need to be mutually exclusive.

Many people will be quick to point out that success doesn't come without hard work and sacrifice. I absolutely believe hard work is part of the success equation, but it's not the sole factor. You will not get a business off the ground without massive effort, but too many men confuse hard work with personal sacrifice, which is where the savior complex starts to take root. You don't have to kill yourself for your family to be happy or for your business to be a success. Sacrifice is a zero-sum game — it implies you are allowed only one outcome: happiness or success. Wealth or a well-rounded family. Making a living or following your dreams.

But that's just not true.

You can have a thriving business and still be fully present with your family. You can make a lot of money and still have the adventures you dream about. At the time of writing this book, Design Pickle is on track to do eight figures in revenue in the next 18 to 24 months. I spend quality time with my family every day, and take my wife and three daughters on weekly dates. We recently returned from a six-week trip to Belize, adventuring together and homeschooling our daughters. And through all of this, my businesses still ran — and grew — while I was away.

Curious how I've built my business to fulfill my life first? Visit soberentrepreneur.com/bonus to access additional content, videos, and how-to guides created to help you design your life exactly as you want it to be.

Professional success is wonderful, but our accomplishments can cast a long shadow over the rest of our lives. Don't forget about your health and family when you are building up that ruthless commitment, or they will be left in the dust.

YOU COME FIRST

Getting sober gives you a competitive advantage in life. At the risk of repeating myself, sobriety is a decision that must be yours to make and to keep. I can't make that decision for you. Neither can your spouse, family, or business partners.

We've discussed creating outcomes focused on business, family, and personal growth, but if alcohol is still in your life, your first target should be to go down the path of sobriety. Keep this simple, and where possible, attach your goal of sobriety to something else that matters to you: it's easier to stick to your guns and not drink when you know, for example, that you want to have more energy each day for your family. When you can see drinking will cause a negative impact on another important area of your life, it's easy to pass.

Any big behavioral shift is only sustainable when you have intrinsic motivation — the change has to be internally driven, from within yourself. If you just have someone looming over your shoulder, forcing you to change, it's not going to be permanent. Eventually you'll resent the pressure, or find a way to rationalize the past behaviors again, and you'll end up back at square one.

Setting concrete targets also stops you from being

overwhelmed by the decision. Your targets give you a road map for navigating your new situation. People who try to go sober without any targets often give up — they want to get from Point A to Point Z, but have no idea how to find Points B and C to help them start moving. Manageable targets create common waypoints for you to follow; all you need to do is show up and do the work to get there.

My mentor, Garrett, often uses a baseball analogy: the players who focus on hitting home runs have the largest strikeout rates. You don't win games from home runs. You win games from repeated base hits. A single base hit is not a sexy thing. It's not exciting to get someone onto first base. But then you get another base hit, and another, and another. Four singles and suddenly you're scoring. When you're starting the journey to sobriety, go for base hits. They aren't sexy. They won't impress anyone. But with enough base hits, you'll find yourself scoring more with less stress and effort.

I first started writing out my targets around 2007. I called my notebook "the magic paper", because every time I wrote these things down, I would accomplish them. It was amazing! It started out with simple, easy things, but over time each target became more complex and ambitious. The whole thing seemed almost too good to be true — targets were getting checked off all the time. It felt like magic, but actually I was becoming more confident and gaining forward momentum.

Knocking off small targets in order to create big change is the secret to every book, article, presentation, seminar, and coaching session that has ever been created on this topic. The only additional tip I will give you is to write down anything you want to achieve. Not type — write, like with a pen and paper. Writing your goals down is game-changing, because it makes them real.

At the same time you're working towards these targets, you can start working on improving how you think and behave in the world, and in the next chapter we're going to explore how you do that.

---

[1] https://www.summitbehavioralhealth.com/resources/articles/what-is-addiction/

CHAPTER FIVE: BEAT THE BLOCK

Every problem I've ever had has been caused by lying.

I was either lying to myself about the reality of a situation, or I was lying to someone else about my behavior or motivation. While lying is pretty normal in childhood and even through your teen years as you test boundaries, lying as an adult causes real problems. For me, the worst of the lies I told myself were about my drinking. I was lying to myself that I wasn't an alcoholic, trying to convince myself I could manage my drinking and still keep a handle on the rest of my life. I was ignoring objective reality, weaving a story around myself that protected me from having to face up to all the difficulties in my life.

When I finally realized that objective reality and "Reality by Russ" were not the same thing, I had a choice to make. I could commit to living in objective reality, to seeing things as they really were... or I could keep hiding in the rose-colored world I had created for myself. I realized that the life I had dreamt of — having a successful business, a thriving marriage, and a happy, healthy family — was available to me in objective reality. The only hope I had to get there was to face up to the false version of reality I had created.

"Reality by Russ" is a prime example of the entrepreneur's paradox. You might have heard of the "reality distortion field" many of us have that allows us to bend the world around us to our will. The concept, made famous by Steve Jobs, is that through hard work, belief, and sheer force of will, we create something out of nothing. We have to believe in ourselves before anyone else will, create results when others can't, and over time we can become masters of selling a rosy story to anyone who will buy it.

For too many of us, myself included, this ability allows us to lie to ourselves *and* everyone around us. We work so hard at believing in the dream that we lose touch with reality. Instead of dealing with our problems as they arise, we push them away, scared deep down that acknowledging our faults and mistakes could turn our whole lives into disaster zones.

Don't get me wrong: being able to sell the vision is an incredibly valuable skill, but our greatest strength can also be our greatest weakness. The problem happens when we start *lying* to ourselves and others about a version of reality that doesn't exist. A strong business thrives on solid foundations: a passionate leadership team, honest financials, and a great product. Within our own lives, the same holds true. When we ignore the hard truths of our reality and choose to tell ourselves that everything is fine, it's only a matter of time before everything comes crashing down.

Ironically, the disasters only happen when we *don't* acknowledge our problems. They simmer away below the surface until something makes them boil over, and suddenly all the fear and doubt and pain comes bursting out at once. Not only do *you* have to pick up the pieces of your shattered reality, but so do all the important people in your life. Your spouse, your kids, your colleagues, and you customers are suddenly thrown into a new, more accurate version of your reality they didn't know about, and the fallout can be devastating.

The Block, as we will call it, is this willful self-delusion that you can have your cake and eat it too. It's the belief that you can build a successful business, have a happy marriage, be fighting fit, *and* keep up your addictive habit of choice.

Spoiler alert: You can't.

The Block is our biggest barrier to growth and success, and no one can pull you through it but yourself. Of the men who have successfully pulled through their own Block, there are three distinct types of breakthrough:

- *Hitting rock bottom*
- *Hearing your inner voice*
- *Shocking your system*

HITTING ROCK BOTTOM

If you've never hit rock bottom before, this is your invitation to keep it that way. Many people have hit it before you, and it's so common among entrepreneurs that I've compiled a list of all the ways it usually goes down. Think of this section as the ultimate life hack: you can see all the ways other people have screwed up their lives before you get to that point yourself, and you can do whatever it takes to stop yourself from hitting that point. Here are some of the most common indicators that you are hurtling towards rock bottom:

- *Destroying a relationship in a spectacular fight*
- *Getting arrested or charged with a crime*

- *Developing a serious health issue*
- *Finding yourself driving under the influence*
- *Sexually promiscuous behavior*
- *Destructive business decisions*

Whatever form rock bottom takes, you realize in a flash of clarity you have royally screwed up, and things can't get any worse. For me, getting caught in the affair was the trigger that finally blew my life up and sent me crashing face-first into rock bottom. My drinking had gotten out of control, my business was floundering, and I was trapped in a crazy prison of my own making. At this point, I was forced to acknowledge that my life was a wreck and I needed to change. It's not an experience I would wish on anyone, but in some ways, hitting rock bottom was a blessing in disguise. I had no choice but to recognize that things had gotten out of control, I'd been lying to myself and others, and I had to change immediately in order to rebuild my life. In AA and Celebrate Recovery meetings, this is a surprisingly common feeling. In a way, rock bottom represents solid ground, and it can help you get your footing in a place that, until then, had been covered up in lies and half-truths. At rock bottom, we can push against something substantial and start swimming up towards the air again.

HEARING YOUR INNER VOICE

Sometimes hitting rock bottom doesn't happen suddenly. Some people sink gradually towards that point, becoming more and more uncomfortable with their situation, but don't change course. You'll know this is you if you occasionally hear a quiet voice in the back of your head or deep in your gut that seems to be warning you of impending doom. If your body is telling you that you're on a collision course, don't push it away or try to rationalize your bad decisions.

Listen. You need to pay attention to that voice.

Your brain is an incredibly perceptive piece of equipment. It comes standard with pattern-recognition software even Tesla and Google haven't been able to replicate. It constantly scans your environment for information and patterns it can use to help you survive and thrive. So when that inner voice starts clamoring in the background that your behavior is reducing your chance of surviving or thriving, pay attention. It's not just self-doubt or the normal entrepreneurial stress. Your brain has identified that you are following a destructive pattern it has seen previously (either from your past or from watching others) and is trying to pull you back from the edge.

If you can heed that inner voice, if you can build up

the courage to face your fear and shame, you can avoid the depths of despair. But if you push that voice aside and ignore all the warning signs, you're in trouble. If you can strip away the story you've been telling yourself and look at reality as it really is, you can save yourself. Please, apply the lessons I learned the hard way to your situation. Deep down, I knew my behaviors were destructive and selfish. I knew I was making bad decisions both in my business and my relationships, but I ignored all the red flags and flashing lights in my brain. I sold myself on a false version of reality, and I paid dearly for it. You have an opportunity now to take a hard look at your life, and to start making positive changes before you face the same destruction.

SHOCKING YOUR SYSTEM

Some of us fall into a third category and never hit rock bottom or hear that profound message from our inner voice; instead we're slapped with a terrible experience after years of coasting. I believe this is the most common and insidious of the three breakthrough situations, and unfortunately it takes the longest, too.

Think about a swimming pool that gets really messed up because the owner doesn't take care of it properly. They neglect it or assume it will take care of itself, and over time the chemical balance gets so screwed up that there's no way you could swim in it. When that happens, a pool repair company will come around and shock the water with chemicals to fix it. For a while, you can't swim in it unless you want chemical burns and nasty scalded skin, but eventually the chemicals dissipate. The water dilutes, the poisonous bacteria die off, and soon enough it's good as new.

Like the pool, people stagnate with time. You can go on indefinitely, not realizing anything is wrong, and then discover one day that the water has turned to acidic green jello. This is what happens to people who achieve a basic level of success and stop pushing themselves to do more.

It's not easy to be successful creating your own professional path. It takes talent and work to be successful, but not an impossible amount. When we get to a comfortable level of success, we often decide (consciously or subconsciously) that we don't want to risk anything more. We are scared ongoing growth could jeopardize the success we've achieved. We're so fearful of going backwards that we decide to stop any forward progress and settle for what we've got. Maybe you can relate — you can afford to go on vacations, have a nice home in a nice suburb, and can go out whenever you want. Life is comfortable. You feel like you've made it, and you don't need to push any harder.

But in reality, when you stop pursuing uncomfortable growth, you stop advancing as an individual. You stop evolving, and this can cause massive problems over time, because things around you *do* change. Your children change. Your spouse changes. Your business partners change. The economy and business environment change. If you're not evolving and improving, the gap between you and everyone around you grows and grows until one day you wake up to divorce papers or a hostile takeover with absolutely no idea how you got there.

I've watched these exact things happen to several friends in the last few years. They were all hard-working, good guys who thought everything was going great, until their wives or business partners dropped a bomb on them. Providing a nice house and a stable environment for your kids is not enough to keep you connected to your family. Maintaining good relationships with existing clients is not enough to keep you in business. If you stop evolving, the world moves on without you, and that's almost worse than bottoming out. At least when you hit rock bottom, you know there's an acute issue, a challenge you can push back against. Getting blindsided by a problem you were totally oblivious to is much harder to recover from.

So ask yourself: are you still growing?

Are you still challenging yourself, doing hard things, reaching for the next level in your life?

Are you still having real, engaged conversations with your spouse, and connecting with them physically?

Are you being proactive in your business, and taking an active interest in your kids?

Or are you coasting?

Have you convinced yourself you deserve to take it easy now that your struggles are behind you?

If you've stopped evolving, consider this your chemical shock: get your ass into gear again, or get ready for a rude awakening.

GETTING PAST THE BLOCK

Once you drop your rosy version of reality and start living in objective reality, there's no limit to what you can create. If you continue to pursue growth and commit to being honest with yourself, your life can change in incredible ways. The single most important decision you can make is to stop lying. Stop lying to yourself, and stop lying to the people around you. No more lying, period. Simple, right?

Simple, but not easy.

It's actually really, really hard. We've all been lying for a long time — sometimes so long that we can't imagine not doing it. When I decided to drop "Reality by Russ" and got really honest with myself and everyone else, a ripple of positive change went through my whole life.

One of the best things that happened was a deeper level of intimacy with my wife (and yes, that meant more sex too). She and I have very different love languages: I like to talk; she does not. She loves gifts; I couldn't care less. We had made a lot of progress around intimacy, but I knew we were not at the highest level we could achieve together. Committing to telling the truth meant we had a whole bunch of conversations around this issue. I was able to talk to her about this normally uncomfortable topic and, as it turns out, she was totally on the same page. Being straightforward dissolved the awkwardness and misunderstanding that used to happen with those conversations, and we were both left clear on what the other person wanted in every part of the relationship.

When I started applying radical truth to my business, it became very obvious where I needed to make changes. Historically, I would dodge or avoid difficult conversations. Now I tackle them head on, regardless of the topic. I strive to lead my teams with unwavering truth about every aspect of the business. Nothing is off-topic or out of bounds.

Now, am I perfect? Not at all. I catch myself reacting with a lie all the time. But the more honest I am, the more frequently I stop and think about what I say to people, the better they respond to me. We live in such an emotionally sensitive culture, where telling the truth doesn't seem to be socially acceptable. But when I live as truthfully as possible, people are grateful, and I live in full integrity.

If you know deep down that it's time to join objective reality, then it's time to let go of the lies and stories you've been wrapped up in. Don't worry about what everyone else thinks. Allow yourself to be uncomfortable. How people respond to you as you evolve is up to them, and you do not have to have peace or equilibrium with everyone at all times, especially if it gets in the way of this critical stage of your growth. It's better to experience a period of discomfort than a lifetime of stagnation or suffering. We'll talk more about how to build that foundation of self-confidence later in this book, but for the time being, think about where you need to be more honest with yourself, and start telling the *truth*.

CHAPTER SIX: SCARCITY

In 2012 and 2013, a psychologist from Princeton and an economist from Harvard published research about a phenomenon they had observed in multiple studies from around the world. Calling it "the scarcity mindset," Eldar Shafir, PhD, and Sendhil Mullainathan, PhD, found that deprivation in any area of life can "wreak havoc on cognition and decision-making."[1]

The scarcity mindset makes you focus obsessively on what you don't have. If you're intensely hungry, you can only think about food. If you're poor and really struggling to make ends meet, you're obsessed with money and how little of it you have. Scarcity creates tunnel vision and rigid thinking when you need flexibility and big-picture thinking the most. The research found that people suffering from a scarcity mindset end up making worse decisions over time, even when they have exactly the same cognitive abilities as people people with an abundance mindset. Shafir and Mullainathan said that "People who look very bad in conditions of scarcity are just as capable as the rest of us when scarcity does not impose itself on their minds."

For many families in the US, scarcity is a constant presence. Money is the most scarce resource, and it can motivate an entrepreneurial youngster to take matters into their own hands and produce as much wealth as they can, by any means possible. In other families, time or love are the scarce resources. Children in these circumstances are directly affected, often for the worse. Regardless of which resource your family was lacking, most of us have experienced scarcity in one way or another. The wounds of those experiences can turn into lifelong scars if we don't consciously work at healing them. A cognitive bias is formed and establishes a set of behaviors that can hold us captive in our personal relationships and professional success.

In my family, we lacked money. My mom is an amazing woman who had an abundance of love, hard work, and patience, but as a single teacher through the 80s and 90s, she was extremely limited financially. She always spoke of money in the context of how little she had, or how much she was able to save. Mom was (and still is) the ultimate bargain hunter. As an adult, I realized that her worldview is focused on limitations, which means that she has always worked incredibly hard just to feel secure. She juggled multiple jobs and worked year-round as a teacher to provide for me and my sister. I am so thankful for my mom and everything she did for our family — she was constantly exposed to the stress of scarcity and did her best to navigate it with my sister and I in tow. Her parents were also very important figures in my life, and they had experienced the impact of the Great Depression first-hand. The generations before me had an intense, hardwired belief that there were very limited resources to go around.

My dad didn't have it much easier. His father died when he was in high school in Morenci, Arizona, leaving him without a role model in an economically depressed area. Dad spent over 30 years as a distributor for a family-owned Pepsi business — delivering sugar water in rural Arizona is not exactly a high-growth, high-opportunity career. Recently, he left Pepsi and decided to pursue teaching, which he has always been passionate about. He told me many times he had to keep his Pepsi job to make enough to support his new family and children from his second marriage, even though he hated it. He spent a huge chunk of his life suppressing who he was in order to get by — another victim of scarcity, locked into the belief that he couldn't take a risk on something he really cared about because he had to hold on tight to what little money he had.

Both sides of my family believed that the only way to get some of the limited wealth in the world was to work yourself into the ground, to sacrifice, to suffer. This belief is pervasive in many families, and I'd be willing to bet that yours was similar. Maybe you'd hear *"Money doesn't grow on trees"* on the days your parents were feeling stressed about money. On other days they might have put a cheerful spin on it — *"the best things in life are free,"* or *"you can't buy happiness!"*

These limiting beliefs that money is scarce, and that you're just one bad break away from disaster, can be pervasive through the rest of your life if you don't deal with them. Many entrepreneurs experience the effects of scarcity for years after they start a business. Scarcity beliefs can create a cascade effect that can lead you to some very dark places: if you have a scarcity mindset about money, you are likely to have huge anxiety about how much money your business makes. When you have that level of anxiety, you don't perform well, so you can end up relying on substances to help you get through every day. I can draw a straight line from my family's sense of scarcity to my relentless drive to build my own businesses, and from there to my drinking problem — I was constantly trying to soothe my anxiety about money and success with alcohol.

Before going sober, I was in a constant state of mental scarcity. I didn't have enough time in the day; I wasn't making enough money; nothing was as good as it could have been. Even worse? I couldn't see how I fixated I was on everything I didn't have — and hangovers didn't make it any easier!

Every time I had to make a business decision, I would agonize about getting it wrong, because I always felt like we were just on the edge of "making it," and was worried that one bad call could ruin the company. I was fearful of regretting my decisions, and even more scared I would miss out on better opportunities.

When I got married, I wanted to create the perfect life for Mika and Maddix. I saw other guys in my industry making fistfuls of cash, and I thought I was at fault, that I wasn't working hard enough, or that I wasn't putting in enough time or giving my business enough attention. I battled uphill with this invisible burden for nearly eight years, weighed down by alcoholism and isolation. Over time my life became a formula for selfishness and confusion. The belief that all the good things in life were limited slowed me down and prevented me from feeling happy, safe, secure, and at peace with myself.

Fortunately, the scarcity mindset is just a mental

pattern that can be updated with time and attention. These days, I don't care what people think or say about me, and I know I'll never have to worry about money again, because I've learned how to see abundance and opportunity.

MOVING FROM SCARCITY TO ABUNDANCE

To escape the scarcity mindset, two things have to happen. First, you have to realize you're suffering from those ingrained beliefs that you picked up from your family and environment. Second, you have to make a plan to gradually unpack the beliefs and replace them with a new model of the world.

If you want to create significant change in any part of your life, the best thing you can do is find someone to hold you accountable. As an entrepreneur, you lack the accountability structures that most people can rely on. You set your own hours, you don't have a boss to answer to, and there's nothing to stop you from taking the business into the stratosphere or off a cliff. This lack of formal accountability may very well have led to some of your more destructive habits, and the only chance you have to get out of your own way is to get some external accountability. Even if you're not self-destructive, accountability can help you create massive momentum.

Accountability can help you on many fronts:

- *Generating ideas to create business growth*
- *Solving recurring or isolated problems in your business or personal life*
- *Avoiding alcohol, substance abuse, or engaging in reckless or addictive behaviors*
- *Correcting a persistent behavior that's no longer serving you*
- *Updating your mindset around a particular issue*
- *Achieving specific tasks on a timeline*
- *Integrating non-work priorities (like health and hobbies) into your life for more balance*

Having another person (or group of people) to hold you responsible for your choices and behavior is incredibly powerful. We all have blind spots, and we're all good at bending reality to what we want it to be — but when you're serious about making a change, you have to step away from those cognitive biases. You are not able to call yourself on your own BS, and without a structured accountability relationship, other people won't either. It's not enough to believe that your spouse or friends will tell you what you need to hear — they can't fill that role for you. While the accountability in those relationships can be powerful, it ultimately has its limitations. Sometimes your spouse or friends are too close to the issues at hand or have been affected in a way that prevents them from seeing your situation objectively.

This is why accountability programs and coaching are so effective. They shine a light on your behavior and thinking without the need to tip-toe around your history or the context of the relationship. If you want to have a drink after a big fight with your business partner, your wife might want to remind you of your commitment to sobriety, but depending on the situation, might be afraid of bringing it up, or she might be overwhelmed with empathy for you. If she doesn't say anything, you can make yourself believe that her silence equals permission, and you end up justifying a behavior you know is destructive.

But if you have that drink, a good coach or the people in your mastermind group will address it head on. They don't care about your *feelings* as much as they care about the commitment you made, and the commitment *they* made to hold you to that standard. A good coach or mastermind will hold you accountable to your commitments. A great coach or mastermind will call you out on your bullshit. A legendary coach or mastermind will help you find your pile of crap yourself and haul it away once and for all.

There are many types of accountability. Each is valuable, and will play a different role in your life at different times. But nowhere is accountability more important than on the road to recovery and overcoming a scarcity mindset to build the life you truly want.

Taylor Pearson, Dena Patton, and Garrett J. White have been my main coaches and sources of accountability. Their programs helped me to get powerful clarity about my history and *why* I had developed a lot of these illogical, limiting beliefs. Once we had identified those patterns and beliefs, we could debunk them with logic and develop new patterns for me to use, more grounded in reality and focused on helping me move forward. They helped me to trust my gut, to listen to the voice inside that knows the way. They helped me create the systems that have allowed me to upgrade every part of my life.

Don't get me wrong — you can definitely grow on your own (and my business book collection is overflowing as evidence of my efforts to change independently). But coaching and accountability is an accelerant. You get external perspective that significantly improves your results. Realizations happen faster and your decision velocity increases. When I worked with Dena, we explored my relationship with my dad from an entirely new point of view. This turned out to be the thread that unravelled all my fears and ingrained beliefs, because it was a weight I had been carrying around, quite literally...

My relationship with my dad has always been tenuous. He and my mom were divorced when I was two, and most of my childhood was spent seeing him during alternate holidays or at extended family events. He lived far away with his new family, and while he wasn't a terrible person, he had a challenging combination of the victim mentality and the scarcity mindset. Things were always someone else's fault, and he never had enough. To top it off, he drank a lot, struggling with alcoholism.

When he was sober, he was also one of the funniest, kindest people I ever spent time with. Growing up I loved talking to him about anything, from his work to stories about his early life in a rural mining town in Arizona.

I never had hate or anger towards him, but I always vowed to be a different person when my time came to be a husband and father. I would not make the same mistakes he made, and I would be fully present with my future family.

During my teens I spent a lot of time visiting my dad during the summers and going to the Pepsi warehouse with him in Payson, Arizona. Every time we went, I spent hours exploring, and often helped drive forklifts and load trucks. Outside, where the trucks would pull in, there was an impressive collection of vintage Pepsi machines that had been replaced by new machines that would accept cash-and-card payments. The old machines were so cool. Some of them dated back to the 1970s, and when I moved into my first house after my freshman year at ASU, I was fixated on getting one of those machines.

After a few phone calls, my dad got the green light for me to get a vending machine to call my own, and I headed up the Beeline Highway with my friend Jim Pedicone to retrieve my gift.

We had no idea how heavy these old machines were. Those things could withstand a nuclear blast — they were completely indestructible. Jimmy and I carefully loaded the machine onto our truck and brought it back to Tempe, AZ. Now that we could get our Miller Lites from a real, old-school vending machine, our college parties had never been so cool. But after a while the novelty faded, and the skyrocketing electric bill soon outweighed the fun of this monstrous extra refrigerator.

As I moved from house to house, and eventually got married and moved in with Mika, I continued to transport the vending machine around. Moving it was no small feat, and eventually the machine ended up in the yard at my buddy's house, where it stayed for several years. I didn't have space for it, and when I finally retrieved the machine in 2014 when we moved to Scottsdale, it was filled with dirt and weeds, ravaged by the elements.

There was no room for it in our place in Scottsdale, and Mika hated the thing. I ended up renting a storage unit just for the vending machine. One day I was having a coaching call with Dena, and she said:

> *"Russ, you've been so focused on not wanting to be your dad, and not wanting to make the same mistakes, because he was an alcoholic and had an affair. He's done all these terrible things... But you have become just like him. Even though you don't want to be anything like him, you're thinking about him all the time, and your subconscious doesn't know any different. Your dad is in your thoughts, in your mind, in your actions, and your behaviors."*

Then I thought about this damn vending machine and realized I had literally been carrying around the baggage of my relationship with my dad for over a decade. The machine was the physical representation of everything I didn't want in my life: the scarcity mindset, the fear of taking a risk, all the bad decisions that could impact a family.

After the call, I cancelled my storage unit and told the property managers about the Pepsi machine inside. I never saw it again, and the huge, million-pounds-of-fearful vending machine was gone.

SOBRIETY COMES FIRST

You can't really tackle your ingrained beliefs about scarcity if you are still drinking. Self-medicating dulls your ability to recognize problems in your life, and so letting go of your substance of choice has to be the first place you seek accountability.

Once you have made the commitment to quit drinking or using any other substance, I strongly recommend going to Alcoholics Anonymous or the Celebrate Recovery program, which is a similar program that developed out of Saddleback Church in California. Again, do this first. Get yourself solid in your sobriety and back on an even keel before you start doing personal development coaching or business masterminding, because you need to be in a good place for those investments to be effective.

I found Celebrate Recovery particularly to be immediately rewarding and supportive, because I felt like I wasn't crazy or alone in my decision — there were plenty of people just like me, with similar lifestyles and priorities, who had also decided to go sober. They weren't at rock bottom; they hadn't ruined their whole lives; they had just recognized that drinking wasn't serving them anymore and decided they were going to let it go. It made me realize that sobriety was just a lifestyle choice, like being vegetarian, and it wasn't going to turn me into a leper cast out by normal society.

If you have tried to quit drinking in the past and struggled to do it on your own, try one of these programs. Quitting drinking solo is a lot like trying to overhaul your diet alone. You can do it, but it's so much easier if you just hire a nutritionist who can teach you what you need to know, guide you through the first few challenges, and then gradually move to the background as you become more capable of handling it all yourself. When you have external accountability, you are also more inclined to make the right decisions to achieve your goals. It helps to solidify your decision — you've made a commitment in public, and you don't want to let those people down.

Once you are solid in your sobriety and feel ready to tackle the next challenge, it's time to find a coach or some other form of personal accountability that will help you build yourself and your business as you overcome any conditioning or scarcity beliefs that might have been holding you back. I am constantly amazed by the number of people out there going through life trying to figure it all out on their own, when it's just not necessary.

There are *billions* of people on this planet, and billions have gone before us. Every problem you face has already been solved, multiple times, and the solution is either written down somewhere or it's walking around in someone's head. Trying to come up with the solution yourself is just poor resource management — it's far more effective to invest in accountability systems that allow you to accelerate change and growth by tapping into someone else's knowledge.

Our lives are measured by our beliefs and habits, and the only way to upgrade your life is to upgrade those beliefs and habits. You can spend years struggling uphill to do that on your own, or you can pay someone to show you the shortcuts.

1:1 COACHING

If you've never been part of an accountability program before, I recommend starting with this format. It's a very tailored personal experience, and sets you up to get results quickly. In this format, you meet with your coach on a regular basis, either in person, on the phone, or online. You talk about your goals, the obstacles you face in achieving them, your mindset, and the various other factors that can play into the outcome. Having someone with external perspective is invaluable — they can see connections you can't, and they have the emotional distance to help you work through things that are too big to handle on your own.

Here is a breakdown of coaching as I have experienced it:

- Find someone who you think knows a lot about life or business
- Pay them money to listen to you talk about your life or business
- Answer their questions about your life or business
- Use the answers to theirs questions to find the solutions you need

It sounds ridiculous — you're basically paying someone to watch you solve your own problems — but coaching has been the single biggest investment of my life, and it has had the largest ROI of anything I've ever done, and I believe it's the most effective way to create substantial, lasting change in a condensed period of time.

Coaching is so powerful because when you are being held to a higher level of accountability, you get what you want faster. My long-time coach Garrett J. White refers to this as compressing time. From 2015 to 2016, I was involved in more coaching and personal development than in all the previous years of my life combined. During this time, I grew my business over 4,000%, built my body into an endurance machine, and signed a contract to purchase my family's dream home. I had tried to do all those things before (and failed), but with the pressure and accountability provided by my coaches, I updated my mindset, found the tools I needed, and was able to hit every one of those goals within 12 months.

My rule of thumb for hiring a coach is simple: work with someone who has already done what you want to do. If you have no idea how to find a coach who would be a good fit for you, ask successful friends and colleagues — they are probably working with someone themselves and will be able to make a personal recommendation. This is the ideal scenario, because while there are various certifications and professional organizations for coaching, anyone can say they are a coach and solicit business whether or not they are really qualified. There are a lot of people out there eager to take your money regurgitating content they found online, so look for someone who has real experience and a good reputation, and can show you their success stories.

Remember that your personal development is the single most important factor in whether you will find success in life. Paying a great coach is one of the best investments you can make, because it turns you into an asset. I have invested in every type of coaching, from a $300 hour-long phone call to a $50,000 year-long program. Every investment has earned me a return of at least double (and in some cases up to 10x) on my investment — measured in real dollars, going into my bank account as a direct result of actions taken from those coaching experiences.

GROUP ACCOUNTABILITY AND MASTERMINDS

You and several like-minded peers meet on a regular basis to discuss the topics the group is focused on.

These meetings typically have a moderator and a regular structure. They can be formal or relaxed, depending on the purpose of the group. Not only are masterminds a great way to build your professional network, but the shared personal experiences provide valuable and diverse viewpoints.

If you're bumping up against a problem in your business, there's a good chance someone else in the group has solved it already — and they can tell you their solution ask you whether you implemented it the following week. If you're struggling to stay on the wagon, you've got a group of supportive people who can check in regularly to keep your spirits up, and who will ask you for an honest account to each week.

———

My first true experience of professional coaching started when I hired Dena Patton in 2014 after attending one of her live events. My life had been through the ringer, and I needed to work through all the trash that had been left in my head. I knew I couldn't do it alone, so I attended Dena's workshop with Mika. When we started working together, Dena helped me to get very real and raw with myself. She helped me to honestly assess where I was and where I wanted to go, and then held me accountable for resolving my inner conflicts and making progress towards the goals I had chosen.

The whole process felt like unlocking life's big cheat code. We straightened out so much stuff together, and I felt like I was playing a magic slot machine that just kept paying out. She helped me unpack the relationship with my dad, showed me how to let go of the scarcity patterns my family had been running, and helped me forge a new path towards abundance.

Once Dena had helped me to clear out my head trash and realize that I could have abundance if I chose, I needed someone who was going to pour gasoline on that fire. I joined Garrett J. White's *Wake Up Warrior* program and have never looked back — it was exactly the accelerant I needed. The program has changed drastically since I started. It's not even a coaching program anymore, because Garrett is evolving even faster than his clients are. He's not sitting back, handing out the same old stuff over and over — he's constantly building something better, and every time I take 10 steps forward, he's 10 steps further ahead.

That's why I've stuck with Garrett for several years now and am continuing to grow in the community he's built. I firmly believe your coaches need to be on the path ahead of you, achieving the things that you want to achieve. There's no sense in working with a coach who makes $40,000 a year doing their calls out of a Starbucks, unless that's the goal you have for your life. If business is your priority, you want to work with a coach who has built the kind of business you're trying to build. If your marriage is your priority, you want to work with a relationship coach who has the kind of relationship you want to have. Those people will be able to provide real insight and experience and pave the way for you. Because—spoiler alert—if you choose someone who hasn't done what you want to do, any advice they give you will be guess work. It might work, but it might not, and "maybe" isn't good enough when you're working on the most important things in your life. Find someone who *knows*, because they've been to the territory before you and made a map.

Working with a coach doesn't have to be a long commitment to be effective. I had two phone calls with Taylor Pearson between working with Dena and Garrett, and those two calls were life changing. My business was literally transformed by two hours of conversation with him, because he had a perspective on efficient business systems that I could never have developed on my own. Coaching doesn't have to be complex, or even expensive, although in my case, the more money I have spent, the better the financial results have been. I think investing a significant amount indicates to my subconscious that this thing is really important, so I put in the work to make sure it pays off.

Some people think of coaching as an expense, but try to think of it as an investment: every dollar you spend on coaching is a dollar you're going to make back several times over. Are you going to spend $10 or are you going to spend $1,000? What are you worth? This shift in perspective is a key indicator that you're moving from that place of scarcity to seeing the abundance around you.

These days I look at how much I'm willing to invest in personal development as a reflection of my self-worth, and as a predictive data point for how much I'm likely to make back from this particular round of coaching. My personal bank account has grown about 500% since I started paying for accountability. Every time I invest more, I earn more. Right now I am on track to increase my net worth to about 1000% of what it was when I started (and the return is easily 10 times more than the amount actually spent on the coaching).

Since getting sober, I have invested over $100,000 in personal development training and coaching. My take-home income has grown 400% and my business has grown 750%... let's just say paying for accountability is far more valuable than paying for a drink!

When we grow individually, we are able to raise up those around us — abundance has a nice way of causing a ripple effect. As a result of Design Pickle's success, I have been able to roll out a generous bonus program for my team. Previously I had never given a bonus in any business, ever — scarcity choked any profits from my past companies. Now, focused on abundance, I am able to share the wealth we create as a team. One team member is even buying a house from the impact of Design Pickle's growth. That blows my mind.

I couldn't be more grateful for what we have built, and we would not have reached this level of growth if I wasn't performing at my peak. I can't perform at my peak unless I'm constantly investing in myself, secure in my belief that I deserve success and that there's plenty of wealth to go around for all of us. It's a virtuous cycle: the more resources and time I invest in myself, the bigger my wins are.

The most powerful thing you can do to move from scarcity to abundance is to get some external accountability. Whether you do that through coaching, or through some other uncomfortable investment where you have to perform, you will rise to the occasion when someone else has an expectation of you. There is the capacity inside us all to achieve that next level, to get rid of all the head trash, and to realize that there's so much more out there. If you are ready to see what's on the other side of scarcity, let's get going.

---

[1] http://www.apa.org/monitor/2014/02/scarcity.aspx

CHAPTER SEVEN: WHO'S ON YOUR BOAT?

Once you've moved yourself past The Block and taken some accountability, it's time to get the other people in your life on board. No one exists in a vacuum, and making big changes will inevitably have an impact on the people around us. Your spouse, children, friends and extended family are going to be affected by your decisions to give up your addictive habit, and by your new commitment to honesty and reality, so it's important to have a strategy in place to help them update their view of you.

When you decide to go sober, it can be overwhelming to think about how you're going to tell everyone in your life about your decision. If drinking has been a big part of your relationships, for example, you might feel people will react negatively. This is a totally normal feeling to have, and it is certainly important to communicate your decision without judgment towards them *or* seeking validation from them. However, most of us imagine that these conversations will be painful, stressful experiences that cause big drama — but in my experience, that's not how it actually plays out.

If the people in your life truly love you and want the best for you, they will not put up resistance to this decision. An occasional complaint? Sure. A *"really, man?"* Absolutely. But the reality is that most people in your circle have probably been affected by your addiction or consumption in a negative way in the past, so this decision will ultimately be well received. Expect varying degrees of skepticism (dependent on the severity of your habits), but if they want you to be happy and healthy (and to have more positive experiences with you), people will be supportive.

One of the biggest struggles around the decision to go sober are the what-if scenarios you think up surrounding your social relationships. Drinking was at the center of my social life, and it was the symbol of having the freedom and lifestyle to do what I wanted. To suddenly go the opposite direction scared the hell out of me. I worried about endless hypothetical reactions and how I would manage upcoming social situations, but the truth was that everything was in my head. My closest friends, who I drank with the most, were absolutely supportive, down to the last man. They're still my best friends, and occasionally we'll reminisce about the drinking days, but every single person who matters in my life has explicitly said how much they love and support who I have become in these sober years.

Occasionally someone who decides to quit will get pushback from their friends or partner, and sadly that's often the sign of an unhealthy, codependent relationship. In that situation, your decision to quit holds up a mirror to the other person's behavior, and they might not be ready to face their own problem yet. Regardless, it takes just one courageous person to confront the issue and help others start making changes. You can be that person in your circle, setting an example for them to look up to over time. While pushback is an unlikely scenario for most, you do have to be clear on what you are willing to give up to get sober. Sometimes you might have to distance yourself from destructive or unsupportive relationships (particularly early on while you are still making the new habit stick), but it's worth it to get your life back on track.

Occasionally, I still miss the ritual of a red wine with a medium-rare filet or trying a local beer in a new city when I'm with people I love, but there's only so much time and so much energy for each day. Whenever I feel a pang of nostalgia or worry that I'm missing out, I know I'm actually getting ahead — all that energy and attention spent on drinking equals lost time and attention given to God, my wife, my kids, my business, and the things that matter the most.

IT'S NOT A LOSS

One of the most important mindset shifts you can have about sobriety is that instead of losing something, you're gaining something. I've heard people trying to get sober worry about not being able to have champagne on New Year's Eve, or not being able to make toasts at a wedding, or being excluded from the camaraderie of social experiences. All they can see is what is being taken away — when in fact, there's everything to be gained.

When you realize how much more you can do sober, how much more perceptive and confident and productive you can be, it becomes clear that you're not losing anything. Even if the only tangible result you gain is being able to get up earlier because you're not hung over, that alone will give you a huge advantage in every part of your life. Anything you want to accomplish becomes more achievable when you're not fighting a hangover or a cloud of regret.

It's not surprising people feel like they're losing something, though. Alcohol sales account for billions of dollars in revenue every year, and companies pour a good chunk of that money back into advertising. The most common themes of those ads? That to celebrate and socialize you have to drink, that alcohol is what makes life fun, and that alcohol makes *you* fun. It's not true, of course, but this is why so many people experience such high levels of anxiety at the idea of going sober.

Every addiction makes you fearful of what you might lose when you give up the habit. If you're at that point with your business, fitness, painkillers, alcohol, or social media, it's time to flip the switch and start thinking about what you would *gain* if you gave it up. Maybe you would get back your time and freedom, so you can pursue new things that energize you. Maybe you would get back your mental clarity and find you're able to solve your problems in ways you never saw before. Maybe you would get your health back. What if you give up the habit and found you weren't trapped in a dysfunctional or unprofitable or demanding business anymore?

Most addictions fill some kind of need in us. At the

core of those needs is the deepest human need of all: to be loved and accepted. We've been programmed to think that alcohol or our other habits go hand in hand with social acceptance, and we're programmed deeply to avoid social exclusion. When you kick your additions to the curb, it's important to build new ways to keep connecting with the people in your life. This can help calm down the prehistoric part of the brain that's freaking out that you might lose your social status, and help you to feel confident that this new chapter of your life is going to be kick-ass.

STARTING FRESH WITH YOUR SPOUSE

On our first date together, Mika and I drank all day. We spent the day bar-hopping, drinking cocktails, and laughing all the way. It was an epic day. While we were dating, and for years after we got married, we would go out for beautiful dinners together and enjoy great wines with our food. We travelled together from San Francisco to New York and many other parts of the world, always trying the traditional offerings of the area. When we visited Japan, we drank sake at a thousand-year-old distillery in rural southern Japan. To give up those experiences with my best friend was certainly one of the most difficult parts of my decision to go sober. Alcohol had always been part of our rituals together, so it was very important to me to navigate this change in our dynamic in a way that would make our bond even stronger.

When I first told Mika I had quit drinking, she was supportive but admittedly skeptical — this wasn't a new conversation. We had talked about me quitting several times before, but I had never followed through on it. We had been working through the aftermath of the affair and we were finally on a path to healing, but I knew if we were going to continue to improve, I had to quit. Mika would never be able to trust me with alcohol still in my life, and while she definitely believed I *could* do it, she wasn't fully convinced that I *would* do it. She was very concerned for me, and even offered to give up drinking in solidarity. I was very grateful, but I also knew her decision would have no impact on whether or not I stuck to my sobriety. I told her *"If you want to quit because you feel it's a habit that doesn't support the life you want, then by all means, do it. But don't quit for me."*

Now, my commitment to our marriage and to becoming a new person far outweighed any temptation to drink, so having alcohol around was not an issue for me. This may not be the case for you, and early on it's best to have the deck stacked in your favor. Removing all alcohol or the addictive substance or behavior of choice is never a bad decision. (I recall Tim Ferriss' journey in *The 4-Hour Work Week*. He was addicted to his business and had to physically ship himself across the world to get clear. The resulting clarity launched his career as an author, so don't be surprised at what comes out of your first few clean months.)

Mika is my number one cheerleader, and when I celebrated my first year of sobriety, something clicked. Her doubt about whether my sobriety would stick melted away. She saw I was fully committed, and this marked a major turning point in rebuilding the trust in our marriage.

Since then, we've worked on creating new rituals and bonding experiences that are fun and energizing to keep us connected. From the start of our relationship, Mika and I connected around fitness, and so we've doubled down on doing physical activities together. We still travel together as much as we can, with and without the kids. Obviously, our family together is a major point of connection, complete with layers of traditions and experiences unfolding every day.

Some of the changes were unexpectedly welcome. I lost weight and my energy went through the roof. Feeling more confident about myself physically increased my self-esteem, which Mika finds attractive and enabled us to connect more physically. Mika has told me on multiple occasions how safe she feels now. She knows that if we go out, I'm in control, and she can relax more because she can trust me to handle anything that comes up.

———

Initially, I didn't want to talk to Mika about all the stresses of work. I didn't want to talk to her about challenges with employees. I didn't want to tell her about accounts receivables, payroll, or taxes. I believed it all was my burden to bear. *I* had chosen to become an entrepreneur, *I* had chosen to expose myself to the risk and volatility of starting a business, and she didn't deserve to be stressed by my choices. But keeping this all to myself isolated me from her in a profound way, because she's a smart lady: she could see I was struggling, and she could see I wasn't going to let her in. Given the chance, she would have been totally supportive and would have helped me get out of my head — maybe I would have gotten enough perspective to change course before I did so much damage. By trying to protect her from my mess, I just made it worse. Learn from my mistake. Your spouse wants you to succeed and is in your corner. Lean on them, allow them to share their strength with you. You'll be able to return the favor down the line, and that give-and-take is what makes a marriage strong over time. Let go of the need to look perfect or to maintain the facade you've built around yourself. Give your partner the honesty they deserve.

These days, talking about my challenges comes much more naturally. It's not stressful to get the words out, and I can loop my family in to get their perspective and support on anything I'm facing. Nothing has to be compartmentalized anymore, and I'm not juggling multiple versions of the truth. I have so much more mental energy now, because I'm not trying to live in a different version of reality with every person, depending on what I've told them.

That's not to say that you should just blurt out every damn thing that comes into your head. There's a difference between being honest and having no boundaries, and this is a key piece of the puzzle when you're rebuilding your life.

Be warned on your new path of honesty: everything in your mind today has been rattling around in there for a long time. You might have been thinking about something for months or years, turning over all the possibilities and nuances. The person on the receiving end has not.

In my experience, suddenly dropping all the pretence without any warning is a recipe for disaster. You've thought about it all for ages, so it doesn't seem shocking to you. But, for the person receiving the information, shocking might be an understatement. When people are shocked they shut down, and you end up with the opposite outcome of what you were trying to achieve: greater isolation between you and them, because they are protecting themselves and are not going to open up again until you back off.

To avoid this, start slowly. There's an appropriate way to start conversations without crushing the other person. Share truths that push boundaries and are significant, but try not to shatter worldviews. Continue to share, moving closer to the whole truth each time. Not everyone will travel along the road with you, but using a gradual approach will ensure they are deciding to part ways for the right reasons, not out of fear or shock.

FIND COUNCIL

Unpacking difficult truths — or unravelling a past filled with lies — is where a counselor, mediator, or therapist can play a powerful role. They know how to pace those conversations appropriately, and if you have big stuff to work through, I can't recommend it enough. Mika and I saw a counselor who worked us through the most painful conversations around my addiction, my affair, and the other problems that had developed in our marriage. He did it in a very safe, structured way that was far more effective than the two of us trying to wing it in our kitchen.

Initially, we would go to the therapist and talk for an hour, and it seemed like we barely scratched the surface. I left the first few sessions thinking that there was so much more we needed to discuss, and that we were wasting our time with this surface-level stuff. In hindsight, he was setting us up for future conversations that would enable us to get deep into difficult territory. He built a solid foundation Mika and I could share, helping us to use new ways of communicating with each other, and new ways of hearing each other. Those early sessions protected us when we got to the heavy topics — coming out the other side better than ever, instead of getting stuck in a meltdown.

Having a third party present also gives both people a sense of boundaries during difficult conversations, and helps you to conduct yourself at a better standard. It stops you both from trying to "win" an argument, and it can stop the knives from coming out. You're far less likely to say something hurtful or untrue when you have an external party present. Mika and I came out of every counseling session content with the conversation — not always *happy*, per se, but it never felt like we were adversaries, or that one person would win and the other would lose. A great mediator or therapist will help you bridge the gap and find a firm common ground to build on.

Of course, there's a lot of stigma about going to counselling. People worry what their friends will think, or feel that they've failed somehow. But what's more important? The success of your marriage, family, and business? Or what someone else thinks? You might be uncomfortable to begin with, but the specter of public opinion and self-doubt will quickly fade as the possibility of a restored marriage and thriving relationships takes shape.

MANAGING FAMILY DYNAMICS

A lot of people drink because they're uncomfortable in raw social situations. It's easy to use alcohol as a crutch to feel bonded to people — without having to have the uncomfortable conversations that actually *make* you bonded. Nowhere is this more obvious than in family gatherings, which can be loaded with destructive history and ingrained behaviors.

When the family dynamic is volatile or difficult, it can be extremely challenging to be present and candid. There's so much that goes unsaid in extended family relationships, and if there's not a family culture of honesty, you can feel trapped and anxious whenever you all get together. It's not surprising, then, that a drink (or five) feels like exactly what you need to get through it all. But when you sedate yourself with alcohol, or bury yourself in your phone, or go off for three-hour workouts to remove yourself from the group, it's only going to make things worse.

Sedating yourself in any way is obvious to the people around you. They can see you're uncomfortable and it makes them defensive — even if they're also sedating themselves. You all might feel better with the added buffer, but really everyone is on a bullet train to the arguments and situations you're trying to avoid. Sedation and self-medication usually end up being catalysts for the very things we are trying to prevent.

As you repeat this avoidance pattern over and over, your 'risk tolerance' for conflict increases, and so does your consumption. You need to drink harder, work harder, train harder, to keep all the mess at bay, and you can end up fracturing your relationships because you're not actually invested in them. As more and more of your energy goes to *not* having difficult interactions, there's less and less left over for actually connecting with your family.

This is a difficult pattern to undo, and for me, it wasn't until I started meditating and practicing mindfulness that I was able to unlock that defense system in myself and get to a deeper level with my family. It was challenging process, but I was set up for success — I had learned new communication strategies during our marriage counseling, and I was pursuing personal development through coaching. Getting into a regular habit of meditation really helped. It allowed me to observe what was happening in a situation without getting emotionally involved, which meant I could make better decisions, which led to better interactions and eventually better relationships.

Now, some families are socially challenging all of the time, and no amount of mindfulness is going to change their behavior. If that's your situation, you don't owe anyone an explanation if you decide to go sober or start behaving in a way that is healthier for you — even if it makes other people uncomfortable. Period. You do not have to roll into Thanksgiving and proclaim *"I am now sober, everyone. No drinks for me."* In fact, if it's just going to make more drama, don't tell them at all.

Apart from Mika and a few close friends, I didn't tell *anyone* I had quit for nearly two years, for two important reasons. First, I wanted to protect myself from the pressure of other people's opinions, and second, I just couldn't be bothered to have the conversation over and over with everyone. I had a great support network and knew I was making the right decision for myself. By the time my sobriety hit the mainstream, the new and improved version of myself had been out for years, which made it much easier for everyone to see how beneficial the decision had been.

On the other hand, it's important to make the conversation about sobriety normal within your immediate family. My eldest daughter, Maddix, is currently 12 years old, and has been asking about why I don't drink anymore. Mika still drinks, and Maddix's mom drinks, and she has noticed that I don't. My conversations with her have been age appropriate, but she gets the truth: I don't drink because I don't like who I become and am not the best dad I can be when I drink. I want our family to be happy and healthy and safe, and abstaining from drinking helps me keep that commitment. As she grows up, that conversation will evolve. One day I expect her to read this book, as will my other children and hopefully my grandchildren. I'm not going to hide my past, because my experience is a teaching opportunity. No one talked to me about alcohol, except a police officer from the D.A.R.E. program when I was in the fifth grade. Mika's parents never spoke to her about substances or addiction either. I am committed to sharing my past so others can benefit from my mistakes.

I'm under no illusion this book will stop my kids from their own future rebellions, but want to show by example that it's okay to talk about difficult things in the Perry family. Everyone should feel safe to discuss the things that make us feel isolated or anxious, the very feelings that lead to destructive behaviors in the first place.

BRING YOUR FRIENDS ALONG

Most adult friendships involve alcohol to some extent. Whether it's having beers out with your buddies or a few glasses of wine together over dinner, it's pretty normal to drink as part of your social routines. You might feel uncomfortable disrupting that status quo with your friends, but the friends who really love you are going to be cool with it. (And if they're not cool with you doing something good for yourself, that's a big warning sign.)

Admittedly, the relationships centered around drinking may fade into the distance over time. I was very fortunate most of my drinking-fueled relationships slowed down and eventually just became great memories. If there is any drama around your decision, or the decision to pursue different social outlets, understand that it's not actually about you. People who challenge you on this decision are highly likely to be struggling with an addiction of their own. Your choice reveals something uncomfortable to them, and it's easier for them to push back on you than to face their own reality.

Many of us drink because we think people expect us to, and we let ourselves get swept up by that wave of social pressure. But you're not breaking some social contract if you choose not to drink, and you certainly don't need to explain yourself to anyone who thinks otherwise.

If you don't feel ready to take on the conversations around quitting, that's perfectly fine. Just tell people you're driving, or that you've got important work tomorrow — I always have work to do and I always drive to events in order to ensure that those reasons are honest. You don't need to give people all the details and rarely will they push — especially after they've had a few drinks themselves.

If you *are* comfortable talking about it, you can use the decision to create more depth in your friendships. I had some very meaningful, interesting conversations with friends when I just came out with it. If someone was giving me heat about having a beer, I would say something like, *"Actually, drinking made me really depressed, I was having fights with my wife, and I just hated it."* Getting real with your emotions and sharing raw truths with someone is a shortcut to getting them to see where you are. People now understand *why* you're making this decision, which makes it easier to digest. There might be an awkward moment while they process the truth-bomb you detonated, then they will ask if it's okay for them to still drink around you, and then life goes on.

That said, the dynamic among your friends will change. You might have to rework your social arrangements, because, frankly, going to bars full of drunk people is not fun. You might enjoy it if you're with close friends or actively dating, but casually meeting someone for a drink or going to happy hour as the sober guy is draining. It's not even about the temptation — it's that drunk people get annoying really fast. They can be hilarious, on occasion, but for me it's far more enjoyable to meet people for a coffee, lunch, or some kind of challenging physical activity we can do together.

These days, I've replaced the connection I used to have with friends over drinking with connections through family and business. We have all grown up a lot, and now my family and business are the clear priorities. I pursue friendships that support those key areas. Many of my friends have also cut down their drinking since I quit. I can't take full credit for that (getting older certainly helps), but my journey has had an extremely positive impact on my life, and I imagine that has been encouraging for anyone in my social circles considering cutting back.

BUSINESS WITHOUT THE BOOZE

Drinking is a huge part of American business culture. At my first job out of college, we worked with a creative agency that would always take us out for dinners and drinks. That was an accepted part of the working relationship — everyone wants to work with people who know how to kick it up a notch! We all want to be wined and dined, and that attitude is common in just about every industry.

When I started my first agency, Keane Creative, I too thought the way to get ahead was to wine and dine clients. It worked for a while — you can keep clients going for quite some time by sheer entertainment — but eventually clients demand results. If you're not doing your job, then it's all for nothing. Performance trumps tasting menus any day of the week.

That realization helped me take a new approach when I started Design Pickle. I decided we were going to be great at doing what we said we would do, and that would be it. We would not be great entertainers, we would not be socialites. We wouldn't sell anyone on anything. We would be confident about who we were and the value we offered. We would work hard to deliver great design to anyone who needed it at a fair price, and that would be it.

It turns out that just doing the work gives you a massive advantage in the business world. Most people use business trips and meetings as an excuse for drinking. If they're drinking on someone else's dime, so much the better — they'll drink more because they're not footing the bill. When other people drink, you have the advantage. You remember more, you're sharper during negotiations, and you're faster and more productive, while everyone else is still fighting off the hangover. Being sober is the Super Mario star in any business environment.

BRINGING IT BACK TO YOUR *WHY*

Getting everyone in my life on board with my sobriety was reasonably easy. I did not experience a lot of pushback or friction, but I've watched other people have *much* more difficult transitions, and I believe the difference lies in *why* you're changing. If you don't have a powerful internal reason to make this decision, then it's all too easy to succumb to external pressures.

My decision was unconditional. I did not do this for anybody else — I did it for me. No external factor will ever crack that resolution, and people don't even try, because they can see that it's so important to me. They can see I'm never going to compromise, so it's easier for them to just get on with their own choices.

But if you're trying to change because…

- *Your significant other told you to*
- *The court told you to*
- *Your business partner told you to*
- *Your pastor told you to*
- *Your friends told you to*
- *The internet told you to*

… it's not going to stick. When things get hard, you'll hate the whole thing and go back to what you know. You need to know your *why*. Know it and hold onto it so tightly that there's nothing that can undo your determination.

I didn't stop drinking until nearly a year after the affair, all the way through the worst part of my life. I didn't stop until I found my *why* and I've never looked back.

CHAPTER EIGHT: A YEAR OF FIRSTS

The first year of being sober is pretty weird. You have a lot of experiences for the first time, again. You've done it all before, but in a completely different way. You'll be experiencing things with total clarity, possibly for the first time in your adult life. In this chapter we're going to cover what to expect as your first year kicks off. And to have a really clear understanding of what's about to go down, you need to have a clear understanding of habits.

Humans are habitual creatures. We live by habit and we love our habits. We rely on them endlessly, often without even realizing it. When we are forced to do without our normal habits, we don't like it, and we feel soothed and back in control as soon as the habit is back in action. This goes far beyond brushing our teeth or waking up at a certain time. Our work life is defined by our habits, and so is our social life. Our habits control where we go, who we see, and what we do.

In many circles, alcohol is a habit. It's a normal, ingrained part of how the group identifies itself and how the group interacts. We never even question whether it's normal to drink, because we all grow up watching our parents drink. If your parents drank with their friends, at family gatherings, and on quiet nights at home, you're going to think it's pretty normal to do the same as you become an adult yourself. As you go through school and college, you're often surrounded by alcohol, especially in countries like America, the UK, and Australia, where there is a strong drinking culture (and being a big drinker is basically how you get your patriot badge). But this inherited drinking habit is really all about the convenience. We want something to do, to be entertained, and so we go out to drink. You don't have to put much thought into the drinking experience — it's easy to get people to meet you at bar. It's much harder to get people to go kayaking or hiking with you, and so we default to what's easy.

When you're single and dating, this convenience feels particularly important. We all think going out drinking is the easiest way to meet someone (despite the fact we've all gone home many times without meeting anyone interesting). But when you quit and become sober, you cut the thread that ties a lot of those social activities together, and you're left to question why you go out at all: what you're hoping to get out of your social life, and how you're going to adapt.

That's why the first year ends up being 'Bizarro World'. You're still participating in a lot of the activities that you did when you were still drinking, but you see them in a whole new light. You still want to be *you*, and do things you enjoy, but you have to learn to do that without the habit that used to tie it all together for you.

You also don't fire all your friends when you quit drinking. You don't cut ties with your family. You don't quit your job. (Well, some people do, if the situation is so severe that they can't be around people who enabled their past behavior, but most of us weren't going out on a bender with our work pals every night. There was just a shared habit centered around drinking together.) But changing the ritual, as we discussed in the last chapter, doesn't have to turn you into a ghost. You can still participate in group events as you work out how to evolve the friendships. That's what I did for the first year. I wasn't quite sure who the new Russ Perry was going to be, so I figured I would keep doing the things I'd enjoyed up until then. That included bachelor party trips, Sunday football, going out to concerts, and the various other activities friends normally do together.

Eventually, I realized that a lot of those things were still pretty awesome… and some of those things, frankly, were miserable.

The activities that sucked the most were the ones that were based exclusively around drinking. If there was nothing else to do but sit around talking nonsense with drunk people, I got over it very quickly. It wasn't that I didn't like those people, but drunk people are drunk people, no matter how you cut it. Not drinking means that you're almost always on your A-game, and spending that mental clarity on drunk people gets pretty annoying. Their priorities in that moment are different from yours; they're thinking about different things; they're acting differently from what you want to be around — it's just not an enjoyable experience. This becomes even more obvious when you start finding activities you really do love doing sober.

One of the things I love most these days is taking a short trip somewhere. When you take a long weekend away and drink the whole time, the time slips and you don't even notice. You stay up late drinking, and then you sleep half the next day. When you do get going, you're sluggish and less likely to actually do the fun stuff you came to do in the first place. The first trip I took sober is burned into my memory, because it was one of the best travel experiences I've ever had. My wife and I flew to Vegas for a whirlwind visit in February 2014 to celebrate our anniversary. Vegas is the antithesis of sobriety. The entire city is engineered for two things: Drinking and gambling—and the more you drink, the more you gamble. While I wasn't worried about falling off the wagon, I wasn't sure I would even enjoy the trip. Normally, you get to your hotel, dump your stuff, and go straight to the bar… which is exactly what we did.

We checked into the Cosmopolitan, went to the bar, had a few beverages together (cocktails for Mika and sparkling water for me), and proceeded to have an incredible night. We had an amazing dinner and saw Britney Spears, which had long been a bucket list event for my wife… and I have no shame in saying the show was *fantastic*. The rest of the night was just as fun, and when I woke up the next morning at 6 a.m. I realized how much I loved the sober Vegas experience. I had no hangover and no regrets. I knew where all my money was (plenty of it donated to the Cosmopolitan craps table), I had time to hit the gym before Mika woke up, and then we enjoyed a great breakfast together, reminiscing about the night before.

Sitting at the gate at McCarran International Airport 24 hours after we arrived, I felt like had been in Las Vegas for a week. I had been fully present for the whole trip. Every hour was accounted for, and my experience was far richer as a result. I hadn't wasted any time trying to find cool bars to drink in, we hadn't waited in long lines to get overpriced drinks, and I had been at my absolute best the whole time.

I recently went on a bachelor party trip in New Orleans and Louisiana. We went to a lake house and fished for a few days. I was up early every day, cooked breakfast, had time to read, meditate, and do my own thing before all the other guys got started. I had an awesome time during the whole trip, because I didn't have to navigate being drunk or hungover (which also meant I didn't have to navigate any long-distance arguments with my wife, unlike several of the other guys). It was a completely different experience from any other bachelor party I had attended through the years, and it was thoroughly enjoyable. This is what you discover during the first sober year: that life is still fun, and often *more* fun than when you were drinking.

I now look at social events as opportunities to do one thing — just experience the event. No longer do I have to plan for driving arrangements, recovery time, a crazy bar tab, or any other curveball that comes up from being drunk. I enjoy the events and experiences for what they are without layering on any complications.

This was odd at first. Socially we are conditioned to want a beer at a concert or a bordeaux with our steaks.

But when you stop, the novelty you used to get from those drinks vanishes, and you start to wonder why you ever cared. You gain so much time and clarity that the temptation to have a drink becomes laughable. These days, I could literally go out every night if I chose to, because my recovery time is zero. Even if I have a late night, the lack of sleep may have an impact — but that's easily solved by strong espresso and getting to bed a little earlier the next night.

Some guys worry that without a drink in hand they're going to vanish into the background of social events. They use alcohol to boost their confidence and presence, and they're scared that without a little liquid courage they won't be fun anymore. My experience has been the opposite. People like me *more* now that I'm sober. I find myself in the center of the action more often, because my brain is on point. I have a lot more interesting conversations, and find myself more relaxed, because I'm not stumbling over myself like I used to when I was drinking.

Admittedly, I'm a social person. I like going out and being around people, and that does make it easier to enjoy social interactions without drinking. But even for people who are more introverted, your ability to enjoy socializing while sober will grow over time. If you've been using alcohol as a social crutch, you will have to summon your courage the first few times you head out, but eventually you'll start to love it. You don't have to worry about how you're going to get home, whether you're going to do something stupid, whether you're going to say something that upsets someone — the fear of all the bad things that can happen with drinking goes away. The likelihood of you screwing up the night drops to nearly zero, so you can relax into the experience, which makes people feel more comfortable with you. You become more enjoyable to be around because you're not trying to control everything that could go wrong.

Now, that's not going to just magically happen. If you really want to become confident, you need to deal with the root of your insecurities. Taking better care of yourself is a great first step — working out, eating well, getting enough sleep — because when you start looking better in the mirror, gaining strength, and feeling more alert and energetic, your confidence will rise.

We all have stories that we believe about ourselves. We construct mental models of who we are and how the world is, but we can change those narratives. How your story unfolds is entirely up to you. You can go on suffering, or you can change. This doesn't apply just to extroverts, either. You can be introverted and confident, just as you can be extroverted and plagued with insecurity. Whatever your current situation, you can be who you are and still have a sense of self-worth. You can be confident in the value you bring to the world and take pride in how you do it. If you're not happy with the stories you tell yourself, your first year of sobriety is your opportunity to start rewriting them. Invest in activities that will help you become the person you want to be, and in time you'll develop more confidence than you ever had with a drink in your hand.

RECONSTRUCTING YOUR ROUTINE

A lot of the peripheral factors around drinking have a net zero value, or will even lead to a loss. At a very basic level, you're spending money — your financial health is being slowly eroded (and if you're into drugs, then you're spending a *lot* of money). Your physical health is damaged, since your organs and metabolism are under a lot of pressure to process a poisonous substance. Your mental health suffers while you deal with the effects of having a depressant in your system, as well as the fallout from bad decisions made while you were drinking. Finally, you lose so much *time* to alcohol. Choosing a bar to visit, traveling there and back, staying out longer than planned, being hungover — it all sucks up your time. In the first year of sobriety you get a clear sense of what truly matters to you, and what you really want to do with the limited time and resources you have available. You get out of the tired old routine and realize how pointless it is to spend time doing things you don't care about. You learn to value your time far more, and so each experience has to positively impact you in some way for it to feel worthwhile.

These days, if an activity won't help me create something, learn something, discover something new or experience something memorable, I'm not doing it. I choose to have experiences that enrich me and make me better, because time is too precious to waste. I've become much more judicious with what I commit to — there are only 24 hours in a day, so if an activity is going to take up part of that time, it had better be worth it. That said, removing alcohol or your substance of choice can leave a vacuum in your life if you don't have something to replace it with right away. It's key to replace that subtractive, damaging habit with an additive, constructive one, or you'll eventually go right back to the old habit.

For some people, getting into art or some other creative pursuit is a really fun, fulfilling thing to start doing when you quit drinking. Music, travel, and volunteering are satisfying options, as is starting a new business, or learning skills that help you open up a new part of your life.

SWEAT AND MEDITATE

You're probably familiar with the concept of compound interest. If you've ever spoken to a financial planner or read a finance book, you'll know about it: small contributions add up over time to create an exponential trajectory. This trajectory can be positive or negative. Drinking creates a negative compounding effect. It's not too bad at the start, but over time you amass a history of mistakes and damage. If you replace drinking with a positive habit, like working out or meditating, you also get a compounding effect, but in this case it will be positive. You get a significant amount of time and energy back, which enables you to invest in the things that matter to you, and over time you will be able to build a history of good decisions and successes.

Alcohol is a common tool for managing stress. It helps take the edge off, and for a lot of entrepreneurs it's the only way they can deal with the psychological strain of creating a business. If that's you, you need to find a method to handle that stress in a more positive way *before* you quit. You need something to focus on during your transition, something that will help you maintain equilibrium and build a sense of calm into your life so that you have something to help you navigate the inevitable stress and challenges that come along.

I dealt with this vacuum by getting more into fitness, and learning to meditate. We'll delve deeper into other ways you can fill the vacuum in the next chapter, but it's really important that you think about how you're going to manage your stress. This is an opportunity to build an interest that you're really into, to break away from the expectations and "normal" behavior around you and try something that makes you feel alive and energized. For me, working out more and learning to meditate gave me so much energy, so much power and focus, that it supercharged every other part of my life. Everything got better that first year, because the subtractive habit was gone and additive behaviors had taken its place.

Choosing an activity or pastime (like a sport or learning a new language) is great for filling the time you would otherwise spend drinking, but you also need to occupy your mind, to rewire the parts that used to be taken up by alcohol or whatever your addiction was. Meditation is your secret weapon.

Meditation doesn't have to be spiritual (though it can be, if that's what works for you). Meditation is exercise for your mind, and is no different from exercising your body. It helps you get better at using your mind purposefully, at being present and fully focused. Developing this skill swung the pendulum for me and helped me stick to my sobriety. More than working out, more than changing my diet, more than fixing my sleep, meditation allowed me to feel happy, present, and calm in my new sober lifestyle.

We're all chasing that sensation of being peaceful and above the fray. We want to be relaxed, and to be able to calm the raging storms that are constantly rolling through our heads. Getting a handle on this in your first year will make everything else in your life easier. Meditation doesn't make the stress go away, and it doesn't turn you into a zen master or stop things from going wrong. It *does* make you better at dealing with it all. You become more adaptable, and you learn to separate your thoughts from your actions. You learn to take a moment to think about how you should respond when something goes wrong, instead of reacting impulsively. Just 10 to 20 minutes a day can create a subtle but solid change in you. Several people have told me that since I started meditating, I seem more relaxed, more confident, and happier, and I have to agree.

If you find something that works better than meditation to help you release stress, calm your mind, and bring you into the present, go for it. I haven't found anything else that works as well, only because meditation is such an easy thing to incorporate into your life. The ROI on 20 minutes of meditation is five to six hours of laser focus. Personally, I haven't experienced a better way to "hack" presence and find a sense of peace in my life.

My mentor Garrett J White always says, "The only wrong form of meditation is no meditation." I personally use Headspace, but there are many apps out there to assist with meditation. Don't forget that it's an endurance activity. Start with five minutes and build up from there. For me, 20 minutes is the right amount, every morning when I get to the office.

USE YOUR TOOLS TO BUILD A NEW PATH

If this new stage of your life is a journey, making the decision to get sober is simply taking the first step out your front door. There's still a long road ahead, and many ways you can travel along it. Filling the vacuum, creating new stories for yourself, using your resources in a new way — all these tools can move you closer to the life you really want. These tools are designed specifically for the craft of building the best version of yourself, and your first year sober is the time to learn how to use them.

To identify who the best version of yourself is for the long term, you need to develop a Decision Filter.

This is a way of thinking clearly about your priorities and behavior, based on who you want to be. If you want to become an industry leader, you can filter your decisions and behavior based on whether they will help you achieve that target. If you know that your aspiration is to conquer a new physical challenge, to grow a business to ten figures, or to build up and coach others, then filtering your decisions becomes easy: Will this decision or action help me to achieve that outcome? Yes or no? A Decision Filter cuts out the gray area — there's only one answer, and so you progress fast and with clarity.

To see a more detailed walkthrough of how I develop and use a Decision Filter in all areas of my life, visit soberentrepreneur.com/bonus

---

The people who struggle the most with sobriety are

those who have nothing else they're working towards. If you believe you've peaked already, that there's no way for you to improve or progress in any area of your life, this is your wake-up call. When you get sober, you find yourself with more money, more time, more energy, and more clarity. You have an opportunity to take every part of your life to a whole new level. Your health and fitness, your relationships, your business, your personal growth — not making use of all these extra resources is a huge waste. Developing a deep sense of purpose (say, joining a church, or building a charitable cause) is powerful, but also a bit daunting. If spiritual ascension isn't on your radar, start with a hobby. We're on earth right now, and we spend a lot of time on earthly things. Focus on something tangible you can put your time and energy into, or you're just going to fall back into your destructive habits.

Once you're balanced, and feel like your life has settled into a positive new routine, then look outwards in ways you can serve. Getting sober is a big deal, and it's fine to focus on yourself as long as you need. In time, you'll find an abundance of time, money, or another resource you can share with the people around you. Sobriety is like a life raft: when you first grab hold, you should hang on like your life truly depends on it. But once you've pulled yourself up and dried off from the storm, you can start pulling other people into the raft, helping them to safety.

CHAPTER NINE: THE FOUR-PART UPGRADE

When I removed drinking from my life, I discovered a huge vacancy — the vacuum we talked about in the last chapter. This new space was scary to face, but it was also incredibly freeing. Once the costs and rituals of drinking were gone, I felt lighter and had more room in my life to pursue whatever I wanted — and it's no different for you. There are four major areas that you can upgrade with your newfound freedom: your health and fitness, your relationships with others, your personal growth and spirituality, and your business. But first, I've got a challenge for you.

Regardless of your physical ability, go on a hike with at least 10-20 additional pounds on your body. Fill a backpack with rocks, or get a really cool black tactical weight vest, and head out for a morning hike. Your body will initially hate having the extra weight on, but after ten minutes or so you'll get used to it.

When you're done with the hike and drop the weight, the pressure of that extra load will become immediately apparent. Losing those few pounds will feel like you just took off fifty. This is the same sensation you can expect when you drop the mental burden of your addiction. Depending on how heavy your metaphorical load was, this positive reaction might be even larger — for some people, the relief is orders of magnitude beyond just taking off a weight vest.

(Of course, this freedom can be overwhelming, and some critics say that support groups like AA serve as a new addiction to fill this void, and it's true that I've met many men and women who became zealots for their support programs. They credit their life and freedom to the work they've done in attendance... Personally, I couldn't care less if those people are now hooked on supporting themselves and helping others in need. Surely it's better to be addicted to a support group than in the clutches of drugs or alcohol.)

When you experience this freedom, the world opens up to you, and you can choose a new path for your life. That's not to say that the path will be easy or immediately satisfying — I had years of selfishness and destruction to repair in my marriage and business, and my relationship with God was nonexistent. My newfound freedom did not mean instant recovery from the challenges caused by years of neglect. My new mental state did not magically change the world around me, and going forward, it would only my actions would matter.

Fair warning: Your patience and commitment to change will be massively tested. Keep your focus on the powerful reasons that made you choose sobriety and take it one day at a time. The biggest triggers of our desire to sedate ourselves come from things we can't control — our business partners, our clients, our kids when they're going bonkers, or the random walk-in guy who gets the Apple appointment before you even though you've been waiting longer *and* you had an appointment.

Ironically, the longer you're sober, the longer the list of uncontrollable items becomes. Fortunately, your ability to handle the curveballs without a drink or other forms of sedation also increases over time, and by removing the temporary escape of an altered state of mind, you can see your challenges for what they are and let go of the things you cannot change.

———

Your habits are the most important factor in success, both in being an entrepreneur and staying sober. We've all seen the articles on the importance of habits and the endless listicles of "the best daily habits for success," but this is not just some clickbait topic. Habits are neural pathways that are worn into our brains as we repeatedly make the same decisions over and over, to the point that they become automatic over time and we stop thinking about what we're doing (for better or worse).

Habits make your life a lot easier if they are additive, and can cause a lot of damage if they are subtractive.They are invisible guideposts that either keep us on the path to what we want or lead us off a cliff to destruction. Drinking can become a habit. You get home; you pour yourself a nice glass of scotch without even thinking about it. You go to a nice steak dinner; you order a full-bodied red wine. The list of habits is endless. How you react to your kids, the workout routines you do, what you wear every day, how you handle your oral hygiene, and so on. Habits are not inherently good or bad. They can, however, improve or erode your life a little bit at a time.

Habits are a pain in the ass to develop, change, and break. There are whole industries that thrive on people's desire to change their habits (and their inability to do so). The society we live in does not make it easy to evolve our habits, and so we have to be on the lookout for the behaviors and habits that steer us wrong. One of my good friends who has been tackling his weight for many years has a great saying: "You can't outrun a donut." Subtractive habits (like sneaking donuts) can far outweigh the progress of an additive habit (like working out). You have to be able to look at yourself clearly and without sugarcoating your behavior, understand what your particular weaknesses are, and build habits over time that protect you from those weaknesses.

Daily repetition is the secret sauce to habit modification. You do the thing every day until it sticks. You know it's a habit when you don't have to think about it much anymore and you don't have to convince yourself to do it — you just get it done. There's no more *"will I, won't I,"* no more arguments or pep talks with yourself in the mirror. It becomes a normal part of your day, like eating or going to work. This is easier when you frame the habit in positive terms. Let's say you want to lose some weight. Instead of saying "I'm not going to eat junk food anymore," reframe the method for achieving your goal in positive language: "I will eat a home-cooked meal every night "or "I'm going to sweat for 30 minutes daily."

My habits got a major upgrade around 2012 when I came across *The Compound Effect* by Darren Hardy.

Every new year until that point, I had always made a list of everything I wanted to achieve in the year ahead. The list would be ridiculously long, ranging from everything from my physical health to my mental development to my business and relationships. Inevitably it would be far too much and I would make very little progress towards any of the goals throughout the year. *The Compound Effect* is about developing just one habit every 90 days or so. Over the course of the year, this can create permanent change in four areas of your life, because you are committing enough time and energy to each new habit to make it stick. Over a number of years, these gradual changes combine to signify a huge evolution from where you started. I still follow this model today, and recommend it to everyone looking to change their habits. You fail at habit change when you try to tackle too much at once. You get overwhelmed and end up changing nothing at all. Success comes through daily actions, repeated over and over, that constantly move you closer to your desired goal. Change doesn't happen in one grand swoop.

Before you move through this chapter, I encourage you to to take an inventory of your habits:

- *What are the habits you want to develop?*
- *What habits do you need to change or remove?*

- *Which of these habits is the most important? Focus on that one for the next 90 days.*
- *What are the small, repeatable actions you need to take every single day to succeed with that habit?*

Repeat this process again in 90 days, and again 90 days after that, and again and again. You'll see how small habit changes add up to big personal growth. The habits I tackled in 2012 were so mundane:

- Floss every day
- Wake up before 5 a.m. (I wasn't naturally an early riser)
- Leave my phone in the kitchen at night
- Make my bed in the morning

You don't need to complicate this. Keep it simple, get a few wins under your belt, and in time you'll be able to tackle more and more complex habits. In the rest of this chapter, we'll be exploring some of the most high-leverage habits you can develop to build success into every part of your life and that will support your journey through sobriety and towards massive growth as an entrepreneur.

BODY: UPGRADE YOUR PHYSICAL HEALTH

Before we jump in here, let me be clear that I'm not a nutritionist, an exercise scientist, or sleep specialist. Everything I share here comes from my own experiences and from watching other people upgrade their health. It's always a good idea to check in with your doctor when you're making big health changes, and to keep in mind that each body has specific needs and responds differently to new stimuli. Try to learn what your body needs and make sure you get professional insight as you go.

Before getting sober, my health was largely influenced by pop culture. All my knowledge came from magazines and blogs that make all their money from serving you ads. I thought that basically all I needed to do was to buy foods marketed as "healthy," pop a few supplements from GNC, and avoid cigarettes. I never considered that drinking was seriously impacting my weight, cholesterol or blood pressure, or that it would neutralize any type of workout I could do.

I realize now that being physically healthy is not complicated, but it does require focus and a little education. You need to sweat every day, avoid eating and drinking processed foods, and get enough sleep.

It's pretty simple, but back then I had no idea how to manage my health, and my drinking was the biggest culprit. I was putting on weight, often felt very tired, and got sick easily. It wasn't until I cut out alcohol that these symptoms of poor health started to subside and made me realize just how unhealthy I had become.

Most of us think that to improve our health, we have to proactively *do* something — eat a specific way, do a particular workout, or change our lifestyle in some way. But when you stop drinking you get healthier automatically. When you quit, the toxic load on your body drops drastically. Your organs no longer have to process the poisonous by-products of alcohol,[1] you don't have to digest all the sugar and preservatives, and your brain and gut don't have to deal with the depressant chemicals that suppress your motivation and willpower. Your sleep quality improves, your cells start absorbing vitamins and minerals more effectively, your immune system starts responding faster, and you reduce your risk of developing heart disease and all major cancers. Within a few weeks you'll be less depressed and anxious, your skin will look healthier, you'll have lost a few pounds, and you'll be more energetic and alert.[2]

DON'T MESS WITH STRESS

I've known a lot of men who drink to moderate their stress. I should know the signs — I was a big-time stress drinker. When I felt anxious, had a rough day, or was thrown into an uncomfortable social situation, I would drink. Over time I conditioned my body and brain to expect alcohol in stressful situations, and eventually became less and less inclined to manage my day sober. I didn't want to face the reality I had created, and alcohol distanced me from the stress. It didn't resolve the problems at all; it just stopped me from feeling it so much. It was about as effective as putting a Band-Aid over an axe wound.

Stress is one of the leading causes of heart attack, stroke, and even cancer, not to mention that it can drive us to the brink of insanity. Stress is a symptom that we're overloaded or not processing our thoughts and feelings effectively. We're not able to control everything going on around us, and being out of control makes us feel anxious, fearful, angry, isolated or inept. This often leads to an inability to control our thoughts — we are haunted by the past and waste our energy catastrophizing about the future.

Stress has a significant impact on your body. It can cause...

- Headaches, chest pain, and muscle tension
- Sleep disruptions and fatigue
- Lowered sex drive
- Digestive problems
- Anxiety and restlessness
- Distractibility and irritability
- Depression
- Self control issues (like bingeing food or substances, or restricting food and overexercising)
- Social difficulties and isolation[3]

When I got sober, I realized I had to find a new outlet for all my stress, like, now. The sources of stress had not been removed from my life. I had not had some huge epiphany that changed my whole life. I was still the same guy, in the same body, in the same business and same family. I had to develop new methods for managing my mind to combat stress, and I had to do it fast. So every day now, I exercise my body. Some days I attend an intense class at my Crossfit box; other days it's a power walk with my youngest daughter, Paige, in her stroller. My goal is to sweat, because perspiration is an indication that I have gone above and beyond the necessary physical requirements for the day and have burned a lot of my stress away.

I do not workout to lose weight. I do not work out to look great in a mankini. I do not work out because it's fun. I work out because it allows me to release a massive amount of stress into the barbells, hiking trail, or whatever else I'm doing. It's like a conduit is opened between my brain and the world that drains all the worries, fears, and negativity out of me.

This clarity allows my mind to go on the offensive. I can think proactively about new ideas, projects, God, or whatever else pops into my head. I can greet these thoughts with optimism, because there's no room to be judgmental when your lungs are burning and your muscles are on fire. I've had some of my biggest revelations during a workout, and I'm not talking about the multi-hour workouts you see fitpros doing on Instagram. If you push yourself hard, you can be done in 30 to 45 minutes. Move fast, lift heavy stuff, push your body to the edge of its ability, and you're good.

I have also tested the best time to work out, and without a doubt, first thing in the morning is the time for me. It's also the hardest, but it gives me the best results. I have tried every hour of the day up to 8 p.m. for working out, but if I get it done between 5:30 a.m. and 6:30 a.m., that gives me the most power for the rest of the day. It makes me far more focused and energetic, and the quality of the workout is also the best. A close second is just before lunch, but with my schedule, that can be a disruptive time of day. If you can't get it done in the morning, I would strongly recommend the pre-lunch session, because it breaks up the day into two powerful halves. You have all the energy in the morning that you normally do when you wake up and get rolling, and then you get a second wind once your workout is done. It gives you a break from any stress you're facing and helps you get some distance so you can come back ready to tackle the problem with fresh energy and focus.

Working out also helps you become a champion sleeper. If you've pushed yourself in the gym, you will be out like a light when it's time to sleep, as exercise tends to burn off all the excess energy that keeps you awake at night. Of course, this is also paired with the change in your biochemistry from removing alcohol. Having a nightcap (or drinking yourself to sleep) might seem like a good idea, but both it's counterproductive. While you might fall asleep faster, your deep sleep cycles (REM sleep) are disrupted by alcohol, which then wrecks the quality of your sleep. You'll be restless and more likely to wake up multiple times throughout the night. Not only that, but alcohol can trigger sleep apnea, which suppresses your breathing and can cause all kinds of health problems over time. Michael Breus,

PhD, a sleep specialist in Scottsdale, Arizona, says: "Alcohol is not an appropriate sleep aid. If you rely on alcohol to fall asleep, recognize that you have a greater likelihood to sleep walk, sleep talk, and have problems with your memory."[4]

Getting good quality sleep is one of the most important things you can do for upgrading your health. It's just as important as eating healthy food and working out. Sleep helps your brain sort the information it collected over the course of the day and form long-term memories. Sleep solidifies new skills you've learned, helps to regulate stress, reduces depression and anxiety, and increases your adaptability and ability to problem-solve. It protects your body from increased risk of diabetes, heart disease, cancer, hormonal imbalances, degenerative diseases, and more.[5] Sleep is the closest thing we have to a fountain of youth, so take advantage of it, especially as your sleep quality improves without the booze.

THE WAKE-UP WINDOW

In 2016 I made my national press debut in the print edition of *The Wall Street Journal*. Peter Shankman, who founded HARO (Help A Reporter Out) tipped me off to a great opportunity to be featured in a piece on waking up early. The journalist wanted to know whether early morning can set you up for success, so I reached out to share the habit that has become the foundation of my day: waking up at 4 am.[6]

To be totally honest, my real wake-up time is usually more of a "wake-up window" ranging from 4 a.m. to 5 a.m., depending on my sleep schedule. The exact time is not important — the real value is in getting up early enough to have focused time alone to get a jump start on the day. This is a habit most peak performers share, and while everyone has different motivations for getting up with the larks, it gives them all an edge.

For me, getting up early in the mornings is very practical, and frankly, it's a survival tactic. I need some me-time before my family gets up and chaos ensues. Some days I get lucky and have more than an hour until my next family member is up. Other days I get 15 minutes before someone is bounding out of bed.

Many entrepreneurs have experienced the chaos of starting the day on someone else's schedule. When you wake up when your family or team is already underway, you're forced to play catch up, which prevents you from focusing on your priorities. If you don't carve out space for yourself every morning, you will be on the defensive for the rest of the day, and can get to the evening feeling like the whole day went to waste. Starting early means that you are in control of the day from the get-go.

Once you've quit drinking, the secret sauce to starting the day early (and feeling good while you do it) is to track your sleep cycles. You could get ten hours of good quality sleep, but if you wake up in the middle of a sleep cycle, you're still going to feel terrible — *timing* your sleep can have a huge impact on how you start the day. Your body goes through 90-minute REM cycles, where your brain waves cycle through different levels of activity (and you'll know if you've woken up in the middle of a sleep cycle, because you'll feel groggy and a bit like you just got punched in the face). This is an easy improvement you can make immediately, as you wait for your body to adjust to sleeping with alcohol messing with the quality of your rest.

A sleep cycle is, on average, a 90-minute cycle of brainwave activity that your brain loops through as you sleep through the night. The more sleep cycles you knock out, the more rest you get. Each cycle helps you to process all the information your brain took in during the day, co learning and memory, flushing out the waste produced by your brain cells as they work, and prioritizing all the stimuli you've been taking in.

There are dozens of sleep timer applications where

you place your iPhone on your mattress, and throughout the night the iPhone's gyroscope approximates the state of your sleep cycles from your movements. The deeper you are in your sleep cycle, the less you toss and turn. As you move around more, you're moving between cycles, so the app can wake you at an opportune moment.

This saves you from experiencing the mid-cycle haymakers that can hit you when you wake up at a static time (say 5:30 am) but vary the time you go to bed each night. The trick is to calculate your morning alarm based on when you're going to bed, measuring it out in 90-minute increments.

Trust the sleep cycle, even if it means getting up weirdly early because completing an extra sleep cycle would mean getting up too late. I'd opt for a 4:30 a.m. start over sleeping an extra 30-60 minutes and being forced out of bed mid-cycle any day.

Now, I prefer not to sleep with my phone in the bedroom, which makes it difficult to rely on an app for the long-term. I'd recommend using it for a few weeks to get used to timing your sleep cycles and getting some useful data about your particular sleep patterns, and then moving to a more low-tech solution — the humble alarm clock. While it seems counterintuitive when every phone has an alarm clock built in, smart phones pummel countless electrons into your retina every second you look at the screen, which stimulates your optic nerve, suppresses melatonin (the sleepy-time chemical), and kicks your brain into high gear thinking and worrying about countless of items.

Assuming you're with me on the sleep cycle bandwagon, the math only works if you fall asleep reasonably quickly. Unplugging from digital stimulus 30 to 60 minutes before bed gives your optic nerve a chance to stop passing along high volumes of data, allowing your brain to slow down too. Eliminate all other screens before bed: TV, iPad, computer, Apple Watches, PlayStation — if it has a screen, shut it down.

Your phone will charge just as effectively in another room, and you can get a great alarm clock that's just as good (if not better) at waking you up for a steal. My personal favorite so far is the RCA digital alarm clock — $11.99 on Amazon. It's specifically designed to tell time and wake you up. There's even a snooze function for the weekends!

DIAL IN YOUR DIET

Overhauling your nutrition also becomes significantly easier when you quit drinking. First, you make terrible food decisions when you're drunk. You're totally impulsive, and your body drives you straight to the foods that have high sugar and fat content, because those foods trigger a reward response in the brain and make you feel good. When you quit drinking, you also quit the 3a.m. Taco Bell and Kentucky Fried Chicken binges.

Second, alcohol has a lot of calories and no useful vitamin or mineral content. Your body gains nothing (except fat) from drinking — even though having a few drinks can give you a day's worth of calories, it won't even give you a fraction of your body's other nutritional needs.

Third, alcohol hijacks the body's fuel source.[7] When you drink, your body uses the acetate found in alcohol for energy instead of existing carbohydrates, fat and proteins. These unused carbohydrates, fat or protein turn into a surplus and end up as fat along the waistline.

On a less scientific level, after I quit drinking I craved sugar more than Charlie inside the Chocolate Factory. Dessert can be a major weakness. Unchecked I can eat multiple desserts in a single sitting to fix my cravings. Obviously this is very counterproductive towards improving my health. My suggestions to curb any sweet tooth include lots of fruit — both fresh and frozen. I've also found a little sweet treat in the afternoon prevents a big binge later in the evening.

Dave Asprey's *The Bulletproof Diet* was game-changing to improve my eating habits — his recipe for morning coffee (basically coffee mixed with grass-fed butter or coconut oil) helped reconfigure when I ate and how much I ate. Having a serving of healthy fats in the morning suppressed my appetite until about lunchtime, which meant I was eating less and making better choices at meals (since I wasn't ravenously hungry).

Reading *The Bulletproof Diet* also taught me to look at what I eat as fuel that will help me to accomplish my goals every day. I can either choose to put high quality fuel into my body and get great energy out of it, or I can choose to put crappy fuel into my body and get crappy energy out if it. How my body feels is now a choice. When I eat well, choosing lean meats, lots of vegetables and water, I'm more focused, more happy, and have more energy for everybody. If I choose to deprioritize good nutrition (as I did recently when travelling with Maddix and had three desserts in one sitting), I will experience some hardcore consequences. I'll be exhausted and falling asleep on the couch by 8:30 p.m., and I'll wake up with a rude sugar hangover — headache, brain fog, nasty mouth, the works.

Obviously, the better your food choices, the better

your body and brain work. This creates a chain reaction in your behavior, too: you eat well, so you feel good about yourself. You want to keep feeling good about yourself, so you go to the gym. You sleep well because you worked out, which means you're more focused and productive at work. Getting your nutrition on point creates a virtuous cycle that can take you from strength to strength. When your body works well, everything else works well.

> *"Real food grows in the ground or has a momma"*
> –Najla Kayyem

Food has become an extremely complicated part of life. Our diet is based on advertising, misinformation, and old, disproven science. A diet that will help you achieve a healthy weight, protect yourself from disease, and feel good every day only requires you to eat real food.

But what's real food? The way I see it, it's food that would exist even if industrial food production vanished. It's the food you could raise or grow in your own backyard, or that you could find out in nature: fruit, vegetables, legumes, nuts, meat, eggs, fish, and whole grains.

Watching a few documentaries about food and

nutrition can give you a lot of insight on this. *Chef's Table* is amazing, and *Food Inc.* will turn you into a vegan for a few weeks. Michael Pollan did a series called *Cooked*, based off his book of the same name. I absolutely loved a conversation he had with Nathan Myhrvold from *Modernist Cuisine* on the dangers of processed and prepared foods. Nutritional content aside, we are simply eating more volumes of food because it's so cheap and easily accessible. Obesity is on the rise worldwide — convenience is becoming deadly.

One of Pollan's key recommendations for healthy eating is to prepare as much of your food from scratch as you can. This helps you avoid all the freaky preservatives and additives in pre-made food, control your portion sizes, and meet your body's nutritional needs by eating natural, seasonally available foods. It also helps you to avoid fixating on every calorie and macronutrient. Nutrition just doesn't have to be that hard: eat when you're hungry, stop when you're full, and learn to tell the difference between hunger and boredom.

Quitting drinking is a massive head start in the health and wellness department. Aside from the caloric reduction, your overall willpower is stronger at meal time. Sober Russ eats salads. Drunk Russ eats everything in sight. It turns out that the hypothalamus (the part of your brain which controls how much you eat), is more responsive to the way food smells after you drink — call it the drunchies.

As I mentioned earlier, your body will crave sugar when you give up alcohol, so be careful not to replace drinking with boxes of Twinkies. You can pass out from both.

If you're feeling adventurous, tackle Tim Ferriss's second book, *The 4-Hour Body*, for an even deeper dive into all areas of health and wellness, from the fundamentals to the fringe sciences.

You might have some major food habits to reprogram, and that's okay. Tackle them one at a time, and don't beat yourself up if you don't get it right all at once. You spent decades developing your current habits; it will take time to develop new ones.

My friend Kraig is one of the top orthopedic surgeons in Arizona and a total hunk. We call him McDreamy. He credits his rock-solid bod to pre-portioned meals: all his lunches and most dinners are prepared in advance so that he has meals ready to eat when hunger strikes. There is no decision making involved when he's hungry. He doesn't have to make a decision about what to eat, or how much of it — all he has to do is open the fridge and dig in. Google "meal prep" to learn how to do this for yourself, or subscribe to a local food delivery service. Call your local gym to see which service they recommend. When your food decisions are made in advance, your health will see an automatic uptick, which facilitates greater effectiveness in every part of your life.

BALANCE: UPGRADE YOUR RELATIONSHIPS

The other sections in this chapter are focused exclusively on *you*, but for sobriety to stick, you'll need to retool your daily foundation to be healthier, happier *and* more connected to the people around you.

Sobriety isn't a magic wand that erases the past and fixes all the problems in your relationships. It *is* the key to unlocking the door to your new life, but there will be obstacles you have to get past before you get to the promised land. Recovering from my affair took almost three years of daily work, as did repairing my professional relationships.

Once you get yourself physically solid — detoxed, sleeping well, eating properly — it is time to work on your relationships. For the context of this book, I assume you are married and have kids or are working towards having those relationships in the future. (If you are committed to riding solo through life, these methods can be easily tweaked for any external relationship.)

Relationship Tool #1: Date Nights

I believe that the secret to a long and happy marriage is a date night every single week. That's it. I could end this chapter here, but I'm worried you won't believe me, so let me explain.

We go through life regenerating every part of our physical body. Our cells generate, divide, die, and repeat the process. You are a completely different organism today from the organism you were at birth — not one cell of your body is the same. This same evolution occurs with our personalities and interests naturally as we age. I am witnessing this first hand in the case of my oldest daughter, Maddix. She is developing new interests and personality traits. She is emerging as a talented creative writer who cares a lot less about stuffed animals than she did a few years ago.

While that change is involuntary, we also experience extensive voluntary change through personal development, whether that's school, coaching, physical training or therapy, and the results depend on your commitment to the desired outcome and the amount of time you invest.

We need to make sure our relationships undergo regular upgrades too, because both people change over time. The man Mika married in 2009 is not the same person she's married to today, and the same goes for me. The 2017 version of Russ would not be interested in marrying the 2009 version of Mika, and 2017 Mika would not be interested in marrying 2009 Russ either. But we've fallen in love with each other again and again, watching each change as it happens, and loving the new person that emerges each time. Date nights are where that happens.

Date nights are not just recreational experiences to get away from the kids. Yes, they should be enjoyable, fun, and creative. But at their core, date nights are a unique opportunity to connect with your partner, and to share who you both are at the present point in time. Change can happen in the blink of an eye — a single conversation, one interaction, reading a timely book. Date nights keep you evolving together, arm in arm, side by side. This focused time protects both of you from being blindsided by changes in the other person that happened when you weren't looking.

The most common cause of divorce is that one or both partners no longer feel romantically connected to their spouse. Both individuals have continued to change, but have not put in the effort to stay connected and to update their perceptions of each other regularly. Don't let that happen to you: schedule one date night every week, and proactively protect that time. Life will try to creep in, but make date night happen and make it count. Do something you both enjoy (grab your local weekly and look up their Best Of edition if you need ideas) but make sure you go deep together for those few hours. Find out what your partner is thinking about, what they are prioritizing, what's challenging them. Stay connected, no matter what.

Relationship Tool #2: Measure What Matters

Entrepreneurs love a good metric. We're all data junkies, and while it's not an obvious solution for improving your relationships, tracking key metrics can make a massive difference. They show you what you're truly prioritizing, what you're crushing, and where you're falling short.

I know one couple — both entrepreneurs, which helps — who have a weekly stand-up on the metrics that matter for their relationship:

- *How many times they had sex*
- *How much their personal and combined finances grew*

- *If they made new social connections or deepened existing relationships*
- *How many workouts and meditations they each did*
- *Whether they spent time deliberately practicing skills they are developing*

This is a couple that knows what matters to them. They communicate a *lot* about what they are prioritizing, and not every couple can manage that. Mika is not a metrics kind of lady. I track these kind of details myself, to keep a finger on the pulse of our relationship, but trying to get her involved just leads to conflict. I tried for years to stick to a budget, based on the all the numbers we had accumulated in the past. I spent so much time on these budgets. I thought about them constantly, always trying to manage every last cent. Mika was always open to it, and could see the value of the exercise, but just would not stick to the plan — it didn't feel important to her. Finally, one night in the summer of 2016 we got on the same page.

We were out on our weekly date night, and boy, was it one for the books. We had a reservation at a nice Italian spot, but we both arrived early, having driven from separate places. We ended up talking about our budget before we got to the restaurant, and it quickly escalated into a big argument. She got so mad she started storming back to her car, determined to leave. I managed to talk her down, and we ended up in a fast food joint near her car — so much for Italian.

Fortunately, a few days before this, my coach Garrett J. White said something that blew me away. He said "Russ, whatever Mika spends, make ten times more. Ten to one is your new ratio. Throw away the budget. Just make more money." When we sat down at the booth, I told her to write down every single expense she could think of — her dream expense list. Eyelash extensions, weekly visit to the nail salon, personal trainer, housekeeper, organic food delivery from a local farm, home maintenance stuff — everything she had ever thought about buying went on the list.

She wrote everything out, I padded the number to give us a margin of safety, and then I put her on a weekly payroll to meet this monthly final amount. The money went into a separate checking account that Mika has sole access to, and we haven't argued about money since. It's been the best thing for our finances, and it's been great for our relationship as a whole. We realized that tracking all our spend was not really important to us — it's much more important that we have a high quality of life and that she and I can enjoy our time together without fighting about something we don't really care about. This frees up all that brain space so that I can track things that *do* really matter to us. I track how much we tithe, how often we're physically connecting, whether we've been going on date nights consistently, whether we've both been working out or meditating, and how we're doing raising our kids.

When these things get missed or deprioritized, there are obvious effects almost immediately. If we're arguing more than normal, or the kids are more stressed than normal, I can look back over the week's data and immediately pinpoint the problem. Either we missed date night, one of us hasn't been working out, or one of us hasn't had the usual amount of time with each of the girls. We both know exactly where the problem is coming from, so we can fix it on the spot.

Tracking the things that are important to you — and ignoring the things that aren't — lets you nip problems in the bud and ensure that your relationships stay healthy and happy. The other person in the relationship doesn't even have to be involved in tracking these metrics, but if you're agreed about what's important to you as a couple (or as friends, or as part of your family), you can be the one responsible for keeping an eye on how things are going.

Relationship Tool #3: Show Your Appreciation

Every day I give something to one of my family members to let them know I love them and am thinking about them. It might be a note in the morning, a text during the day, a small gift, a flower — I believe that repeated acts of gratitude and appreciation go a very long way to building strong, resilient relationships.

These gestures do not need to be grandiose. In fact, it's better to keep them small and simple. This practice reminds you daily of how lucky you are to have these people in your life, and amplifies the gratitude you feel for your life. It makes you feel good about the relationship, it makes them feel good about the relationship, and it creates regular opportunities to connect with each other. It helps you to drop your expectations, too — since you are committed to making a daily gesture and they are not, you can let go of the need to get something in return every time. Anything you do get back is an unexpected bonus, and you learn to invest in the relationship just because you truly care for that person.

This is another reason I love getting up early. My daughter, Reese, is often up by 5:30 a.m. It was her fifth birthday recently, and to be awake when she climbed out of bed to see the birthday decorations we put up the night before was priceless. I had such a clear moment of insight that morning — I would have never been able to do that for her if I had been drinking the night before. She would have woken me up, disappointed that nothing was happening yet for her big day. I would have missed an opportunity to make her feel loved.

Beyond making these concrete gestures each day, the ability to be fully present with your family (or your chosen family) is a gesture that has a powerful impact on your relationships too. People feel seen and valued when you are "all there" — not hungover, not distracted by your phone, not stuck in your head about some problem. It shows them that they are a priority to you, so they feel more confident in the relationship, more engaged, and more invested themselves.

BEING: UPGRADE YOUR PERSONAL GROWTH

The compromises you make with yourself to maintain a drinking lifestyle can erode your sense of self over time. Drinking inevitably lowers your inhibitions, and lowers your cognitive speed. It silences your inner critic, which is why people love to drink. They can feel more relaxed and more courageous and like they're more fun, but there's a trade-off. Enabling those behaviors means disabling other behaviors — specifically, the restraint, self-efficacy, and clarity of thought that help you grow over the long term.

The implications of that trade-off are significant. Instead of doing the hard work that's required to become an interesting person, we rely on alcohol to make us interesting. It has the opposite effect to what we actually want, because we're only confident and interesting as long as we're drinking — our "charms" wear off when the alcohol does. Not only that, but it leaves us feeling worse about ourselves than when we started. We come crashing back down to earth, and on top of the hangover we feel like we're boring, annoying imposters who have no self control, and so the cycle starts again.

Working on yourself is infinitely easier when alcohol is not involved. When we stop drinking, we can develop self-confidence and courage that comes solely from within, and doesn't go away after a few hours. We maintain our cognitive ability, so we learn to trust ourselves more. We maintain our judgement, so we save ourselves (and others) from getting into situations that would compromise us. We maintain our clarity and reflexes, so we are more able to respond to the environment around us. You can do everything you would do if you were drinking, but you do it better.

You might not believe right now that you can do this. Again, it's a question of rewriting the stories you tell yourself about who you are. I'll be honest — this is hard work. It's uncomfortable and it takes time. There is no quick fix for repairing a lifetime of doubting yourself, feeling worthless, or seeking validation. This is not the path for you if you are lazy or unwilling to be uncomfortable, and this is why your motivation to change has to come from within, not from an external source. If you are trying to change for someone else, the motivation to change will not be strong enough to carry you past all the challenges you'll face along the way. Only a deep intrinsic motivation will be enough.

DO MORE WITH MEDITATION

Most people suck at controlling their thoughts. There's no judgement in that statement — I'm still learning to do it myself. Thoughts can run wild when we are left alone with ourselves, and thinking can become a chaotic tangle that wastes the brain's incredible capacity for problem-solving and idea creation. Your thoughts will never go away, so learning to leverage *how* you think is an incredibly valuable skill, and that's where meditation comes in.

Pop culture sometimes portrays meditation as a mystical experience where the modern monk sits on a golden cushion and recites mysterious mantras, engulfed in a cloud of essential oils. Of course, that's an exaggeration, but pop culture does give us an inaccurate picture of what meditation really is. Meditation is simple: it's exercise for your brain. It's not about limiting or eliminating your thoughts, but learning how to observe and categorize your thoughts without being controlled by them. It's about learning to be present wherever you are *despite* all the thoughts coming and going.

Your brain does a lot awesome things — particularly running all the biological systems you need to survive, on autopilot. However, we also use our brains for conscious, focused cognitive processing, where the mind is actively engaged in a line of thought. For example, most of us easily pay attention to things that are stimulating and right in front of us. It's much harder to concentrate exclusively on solving a difficult problem for several hours — that requires honed, clear thinking and a much deeper focus than we normally experience.

When the desired outcome (such as solving a hard problem) cannot be achieved with our current cognitive competence (because we haven't tried to sit still for hours at a time and focus on one thing), we need to practice. Meditation allows us to practice this skill in manageable chunks of time — just 10 to 15 minutes a day can be enough to improve our cognitive performance. Meditation helps us to clarify our thinking, organize our mental frameworks effectively, and examine our thoughts more objectively. That gives us an edge in every situation, because our brains are more able to perceive reality and respond quickly and effectively.

Stress is the physiological response to our thoughts. Those might be incidental thoughts (*"That guy cut me off driving 100 miles an hour! Jerk!"*) or they might be habitual thoughts (*"Damn, I have a lot to do today. Where's my coffee?"*). Either way, the thoughts can latch hold and wreak havoc: blood pressure rises, field of focus narrows, body and mind tense up. Meditation allows us to intercept those thoughts before our biology can respond. We can recognize them for what they are (anger, frustration, anxiety) and let the thought pass by without doing us damage.

So how do you meditate? There are any number of methods — and the only wrong way to meditate is not to meditate, as my coach Garrett J. White always says. There's mindfulness meditation, vipassana, Transcendental, loving kindness meditation, mantra meditation... the list goes on, and finding the one that works for you is often as simple as just trying each method for a couple of sessions. There are apps too, and for many of us, these are the easiest option.

I meditate 20 minutes a day as soon as I get to my office, using the *Headspace* app, which has a great free intro pack to help you get started. If you have no idea where to begin, start with Headspace or one of the other big meditation apps (*Calm* is also very popular). Mika — who was initially skeptical of meditation — practices nightly now to help her fall asleep. She uses the Calm app paired with wireless headphones, and it's really helped her manage her own stress.

JOURNALING & GRATITUDE

Here's something to bend your mind a little: All the religious texts studied around the world are just the journals of dead guys. Now, depending on your particular beliefs, these dead guys hold a little more weight than your average Joseph, but one day they started writing down their thoughts, visions, ideas, and perhaps in some cases, the divine word of God.

Your ideas and thoughts matter. Will you channel God's will and create the next major religious movement? Probably not (please save me a spot in your new world order if you do), but writing serves a very practical purpose. When you write you create a connection between the physical world and your inner world. The electrical impulses travelling along your synapses are transformed into words and ideas, and transformed into physical matter as they become ink on a page: writing turns your thoughts and ideas into reality. How you drive that reality forward depends on what you've written down, but that physical manifestation of your idea is the lead domino for everything else.

After listening to Elon Musk's biography as an audiobook during recent workouts, I'm absolutely convinced that writing things down *works*. His company, SpaceX, is turning the aerospace industry on its head with their lean, startup approach to an industry entrenched in cronyism and inefficiency. His ultimate life goal is to turn humanity into an interplanetary species, and while it seems like an insane idea on the surface, he has thousands of people working on it every day. SpaceX really got its start during a flight when Musk wrote down his thoughts and a potential financial model that would enable the team to build rockets cheaper than they could buy them. That idea couldn't come to fruition until it had been physically teased out of his head — the process of writing it down clarified the idea and turned it into a concrete possibility, integrating key pieces of information that had previously been shut off from each other in different parts of his brain. The solution only came together as he started writing.

I journal every day. Sometimes I write long-form stream of consciousness about my ideas, feelings, and experiences. Other times it's strategic, mapping out a financial model or a marketing campaign. I'm currently writing about my thoughts on writing (so meta). I frequently write notes to Mika and the girls sharing how I much I love them. It's just writing. Don't make excuses or complicate it. Just take the stuff that's in your brain and write it down on paper. It makes a surprising difference to your mental clarity.

2000 years ago, writing was a pain in the ass. First, people had to make a Herculean effort just to work out *how* to write. If they succeeded at this, then they had to purchase the raw materials to physically write: Egyptians and many other ancient cultures *carved their writing into blocks of stone* to communicate their thoughts. That is hardcore, so I don't want to hear any complaining about how hard writing is. Respect the miraculous fact that writing exists at all and take advantage of how blessed we are that it's so damn easy today.

One particular form of writing with a powerful long-term effect (and that's very easy) is starting a gratitude journal. Write down what you're grateful for, every day. That's it. There's no extra credit for creativity or deep emotional meaning in your gratitude journal — as long as it's genuine, your entry can be as simple as expressing thanks for being alive, your sobriety, or a beautiful sunset. You don't have to share your entries with anyone, but remembering every day how much we have to be thankful for is incredibly powerful.

Even if you're in the depths of despair, finding daily gratitude will improve your outlook on life bit by bit. Berkeley University recently published the following finding:

"People who practice gratitude consistently report a host of benefits:

- *Stronger immune systems and lower blood pressure;*
- *Higher levels of positive emotions;*
- *More joy, optimism, and happiness;*
- *Acting with more generosity and compassion;*
- *Feeling less lonely and isolated."*[8]

The more you practice gratitude, the more you find to be grateful for. It's a virtuous upward cycle that lifts every part of your life.

Another significant part of upgrading your personal growth is addressing your spiritual life. Everyone will come at this from different perspectives, and I'm not here to preach or try to convert you to my way of doing things, but all of us have a deep-seated need to be connected to something greater than ourselves. Coming from a secular community and the entrepreneurial culture of facts and logic, this can be hard to acknowledge, but I believe this unfulfilled spiritual need is the root of the isolation and self-doubt that plagues so many of us. Humans have had spiritual traditions since the dawn of time. We have always wondered about "what's out there," what the best way to live is, and what the meaning of life is. Those are questions that can be answered only when you start believing in something.

When I stopped drinking I realized that there is an incredible universe out there, and I do believe there is a higher power behind it. There are hundreds of different religions, spiritual practices, and philosophies, each with a different interpretation of the world and standards to live by. I chose to become an active Christian: I was raised in the Presbyterian church, but I still consider myself very young on this path. The connection I'd had to God and spirituality in my youth had been muted when I was drinking heavily: I felt no connection to God or a higher power.

These days I love my belief in Christianity and am enriched by the work of theologians like C.S. Lewis and William Barclay. Studying their work provides me with a deep sense of passion for life and an understanding of Jesus, and it helps me to be present more consistently. It has enabled me to experience what each day brings at a much deeper level. It's like an upgraded lens that my life is filtered through, and I love that. I love to learn about the Bible and Christianity from people whose lives are dedicated to decoding the Bible, rather than treating the teachings as my daily pep talk. I want to understand the underlying meaning of the teachings, the hard stuff that's going to challenge me and make me look inside myself and grow every day. My spiritual journey is a daily opportunity to learn who Jesus is, what his relationship is to God and humanity. I don't have clear answers to every question, and I will never be perfect (no one is), but Christianity is a framework that helps me live a richer life and make sense of the world.

BUSINESS: UPGRADE YOUR WORK LIFE

Before starting Design Pickle, work had always felt like I was living in a savings bond. It was this boring institution I had to drudge through so that there would be some payoff down the road. Even though I opted out of the traditional employment path very early, I still had the mindset that everything had to be done a certain way, and that it was going to be hard the whole time I worked on it. The guys who run the Tropical MBA Podcast have nailed this problem — you grind out 20, 30, 40 years of soul-destroying work in the hopes of having a nice life and fun retirement, when you could actually be having a great life — with the travel, toys and time off — right now if you focused on building your business the right way.

When I got started, I modeled my agencies on guys who had been in the game for 10 or 15 years and had it all worked out. I thought that I would have to grind for about a decade before seeing any reward, and never thought about whether there might be a smarter way. It never even occurred to me that I could create a business that would make real money right out of the gate, or that it could be fun and flexible enough to support that lifestyle I wanted.

When I started listening to the TMBA podcast, it

blew my mind. After my experience with agencies — the grueling hours, endless conflicts and roller coaster of revenue — I took a step back to work out how to turn a business into a positive part of my life. The last few years had been so hard, so if I was going to start something new, I couldn't go down that destructive path again. That was part of my new Decision Filter: will this action or choice help me and my family have the life we want? Or will it start a chain reaction of negative consequences? Using this Decision Filter, Design Pickle grew to seven figures of revenue within 15 months. As I showed in Chapter Four, it all started with a very pragmatic approach to the changes I wanted to make in my relationship with my work. Just as in any area of life, building a strong foundation in line with a clear goal for the future allows you to build something great. Alcohol and drugs can prevent you from creating that strong foundation, and I see so many entrepreneurs dealing with problems day-to-day and week-to-week, because they're working from a weak foundation, exacerbated by their drinking.

Can you create big things and still drink? Absolutely. Can you create big things if you have a full-blown addiction? Of course. But again, you're living life on hard mode. You're choosing a life with a lot more variables to manage, which inevitably causes more stress. You have fights and problems and fires to put out, and soon enough your words and actions are coming back to haunt you. Why not reduce the amount of complexity in your life, so that when things go wrong, you don't have to put yourself through the same old interrogation: *"Was it because I was drunk? Did I drop the ball on this because I was hungover? Could I have saved this if I was firing on all cylinders?"*

I look back at my agency life, and I wonder what we could've accomplished if I'd had a healthier lifestyle. I will never have that sense of doubt and regret about Design Pickle. If something goes wrong with Design Pickle, I won't have any personal guilt about it — these days problems only arise when a product, process, or person isn't handled the right way, not because I'm hungover or depressed. I still make mistakes, of course, but these days they're honest mistakes that I couldn't have foreseen — not mistakes that come out of being drunk, hungover, exhausted, or not present.

Knowing that Design Pickle had to serve my family and I in a very specific way, the business was designed for success from the very beginning. For me to put in the hours, maintain a healthy family, go on date nights every week, work out, and see my friends would have been impossible if I was still drinking. I spent eight and a half years trying to build businesses that yielded zero profit; now in less than two years Design Pickle is making more money (by orders of magnitude) than the previous businesses ever made, combined. I have significantly improved my relationships with my kids, my wife, my friends, and my team. There is an unquestionable correlation between intentionally building my foundation and the incredible outcomes I've had these past few years.

My vision is to change lives through creative solutions and software, and to do so in a way that allows me and my family to continue to embrace new knowledge, new experiences, and new abilities. That's what motivates me to work, and my business has been engineered from day one to support these outcomes.

If you're looking for a comprehensive framework for everything I've discussed in this chapter, check out WakeUpWarrior.com. While I was already practicing many of the habits listed in this chapter, Wake Up Warrior is clear, concrete and proven model to pull all of these together and expand in the four areas of life we've discussed: Body, Being, Balance and Business. I cannot recommend this organization enough to jumpstart massive change in all of these areas!

Full credit goes to Wake Up Warrior for the Body, Being, Balance, Business concept.

---

[1] https://www.theguardian.com/science/2011/mar/07/safe-level-alcohol-consumption

[2] https://www.drinkaware.co.uk/advice/how-to-reduce-your-drinking/how-to-cut-down/what-to-expect-when-you-stop-drinking/

[3] http://www.mayoclinic.org/healthy-lifestyle/stress-management/in-depth/stress-symptoms/art-20050987

[4] http://www.webmd.com/sleep-disorders/news/20130118/alcohol-sleep#1

[5] https://www.nhlbi.nih.gov/health/health-topics/topics/sdd/why

[6] https://www.wsj.com/articles/why-4-a-m-is-the-most-productive-hour-1471971861

[7] https://greenfieldfitnesssystems.com/article-archive/how-alcohol-makes-you-fat/

[8] https://greenfieldfitnesssystems.com/article-archive/how-alcohol-makes-you-fat/

CHAPTER TEN: BRINGING IT HOME

Addiction thrives in secret. No matter what you're hooked on — booze or business, uppers or downers — if you don't talk about it, it owns you. If you've realized while reading this book that you have a problem with something in your life, the problem will only get worse if you isolate yourself and try to handle it alone. Whether you're staying at the office longer, trying to grit it out on your own, or sitting up late with a bottle of something trying to force yourself to find a solution, that's the warning sign: you're opening a door that leads to destruction. Bottling up your stress, fear, or self-doubt can cause addictive behaviors in even the most balanced people. Self-medicating or submerging yourself in trying to solve the problem solo is only going to push you further out to sea, so please: if you've got a problem, any kind of problem, talk to someone you trust about it *today*.

When we isolate ourselves and get tangled up in our our own minds, we soon believe that our problems are much worse than they really are, and we lose the ability to make good decisions. We become reactionary and go into straight back into that scarcity mindset. The brain is capable of convincing you that you're facing impending doom, even when there's a way out.Trying to handle it alone is how good, smart people end up in terrible situations. Whether they have an affair, steal money from their company, or make some other bad decision, they've somehow convinced themselves that those behaviors are better than the alternative — confronting the truth and dealing with their issues head on. That's always false, and it's a defensive lie your brain has generated in hopes of protecting you from pain, but it never pans out how you want it to.

Externalizing your emotions and thoughts is the only way to stop them from taking on a life of their own and becoming unmanageable. If the only thing this book does is to help you start talking to the people around you about what's happening in your life, it's a huge success. If it helps just one person circumvent the horror of addiction or depression, or find a healthy, constructive way to manage their stress, my job is done.

If you're feeling stressed at the moment, and thinking about drinking more than normal, now is your opportunity to turn over a new page in your life. Talk to your wife, or a trusted friend.

Once you've called someone and told them how you're feeling, go to the gym. Do a meditation and then go to a group class if you like them, go lift something really heavy, or go for a run. Try releasing your stress in other ways and then reassess how you're feeling. And remember: talk it out. Tell the important people in your life what you're experiencing — a burden shared is a burden halved.

When it comes to handling stress in a constructive way, the best defense is a good offense. Build up your peer network and find an accountability system that works for you. Find yourself with an outlet, and do it before you get into a destructive behavior you can't get out of.

———

You might be afraid that letting go of a substance you've been depending on will change your life completely, that everything you know and love will go away, and I don't want to shy away from that fear. Yes, there will be a chain reaction of events throughout your life as you start to confront your problems. But it's going to be a chain reaction that is ultimately positive. Everything in your life thus far has been shaped by your relationship to this substance, whether it's alcohol, a drug, or the chemical high of solving endless problems in your business. Your work, your relationships, your self-perception — all of them have been tinted by this addiction.

The things that fall away from your life at this point are the things that were right for the addict. If you have to find a new role because your business does not support your sobriety, that work was right for the addict, and it's not right for someone who is sober. If your relationships disintegrate because those people don't support this change in your lifestyle, you can let those relationships go, safe in the knowledge that healthier, supportive relationships will blossom in their place. Change will happen, but it's not something to be afraid of. Some of the change might be painful, but they're growing pains, and you'll be far stronger and self-confident when you come out the other side.

It's also common to experience a fear of missing out, to worry that you're not going to have any fun anymore. But I have yet to find a single person who would trade their new sober life for their days of drinking. No one would go back, ever, because they have seen the riches, growth, and clarity that comes from this change. You might miss out on being drunk and having that hazy kind of fun, but you get to have fun in whole new ways — where your brain is firing on all cylinders and you can run rings around every situation.

But more importantly, I believe that the fear of missing out is really a fear of who you could become. When you're fully in control of your life, you can become anyone you choose to be. You can achieve anything you decide is important to you.... and many of us are afraid of that freedom. It's easier to stay in an addiction, to stay small and inconsequential, than to take big swings at life and risk failing. Despite the pain and suffering that addiction causes, it can be more comfortable than facing the endless possibilities of freedom. Being free — truly free to choose your own path — is surprisingly comforting. You realize that you almost have a responsibility to do bigger things, just because you can. You're way out in front of most of the population, and have a real opportunity to change things for the better on a large scale. It's exhilarating and terrifying all at once.

Fortunately, becoming sober can also soothe that fear. All the people I know who have quit drinking talk about the sense of peace that has washed over their whole lives: peace with themselves, peace with the people around them, peace with God, peace in how they experience the world at large. You get this overwhelming sense of calm once your sobriety is established. Your sense of happiness and personal fulfillment increases, and you get to live a much better life because you become able to pursue the things that truly make you happy. The more wealth you create, the more impact you can have on the world around you, which creates another virtuous cycle. You feel good, so you do good. Doing good makes you feel good, so you do more good.

I want to leave you with a portrait of my life now that I'm sober. Compared to the overweight, broke, lonely guy who was pushing everyone away a few years ago, things could not be more different. I don't say any of this to boast, but to leave you with a clear demonstration of how powerful quitting your addiction can be. Your life could undergo the same degree of transformation, even if things are going okay right now.

On a personal level, my marriage is kicking ass. Mika and I have an incredible partnership together — we are having better, deeper conversations than ever before, our physical connection is on fire, and we've built a powerful spiritual connection that I never expected. We had another child, which wouldn't have been possible if

I was still drinking, and Paige has brought a whole new level of joy to our family. Our family is profitable, amassing wealth at a steady rate, building our dream home, and traveling internationally together on a regular basis.

Spiritually I have grown more these past few years than I had in nearly 30 years before that. This has given me a deep sense of purpose throughout my life, and has helped me to build a strong sense of who I am and who I want to become. The combination of spirituality and sobriety has given me the right mindset to pursue the things that are important to me and my family, and has given me a launchpad to help other people. Recently I launched a Celebrate Recovery group at my local church, and being in a place to facilitate that change and growth for others has given me an incredible sense of fulfillment. It will be a powerful source of motivation to maintain my own growth over the years to come.

In the business arena, Design Pickle was launched in 2015. In 2017 we will generate close to five million dollars in revenue, far beyond anything I achieved in the eight years of running my agencies. We will have delivered world-class material to thousands of clients, signing off on over 100,000 unique design jobs. At the time of writing, I have 75 staff, distributed around the world. The business runs on clearly defined processes, which prevents bottlenecks and big mistakes. Day-to-day operations are so smooth that I spent six weeks living in Belize with shoddy internet and nothing went wrong. The company really does run on its own.

These days, my health is rock solid. I am sleeping better than ever before, working out five times a week, and consistently increasing my strength and skills. I have competed in The World's Toughest Mudder — an extreme obstacle race where you complete the course as many times as you can in 24 hours. You don't sleep for the duration, and I did over 50 miles running, climbing, and crawling. I ran my first half-marathon recently, and soon I'll start horseback riding lesson with my sights set on playing polo here in Arizona. I'm lean, my biomarkers are all in the optimal ranges, and I feel energized every day. I couldn't ask to be in better health.

You can be in the same position if you choose to make the change. Take an honest assessment of where you want to be in the next 30 days, 90 days, six months, year, three years. At each milestone, ask yourself: is drinking going to help me achieve this? Am I more or less likely to reach my goals if I maintain my current lifestyle? If alcohol is getting in the way — and if you've made it all the way through to this point of the book, it probably is —make a plan to get rid of it. How you do it is up to you. You can join a program, find a therapist or counsellor to help you quit, or get yourself into an accountability group, but your approach should be determined by taking a hard look at how bad the problem really is. If you're at (or approaching) rock bottom, go to a recovery program. If you're floating through life in a stagnant haze, a coach or accountability group will help jolt you out of it. Set a date night with your significant other to lay all this out for them and involve them in the process. All you have to do when you put this book down is take the next step. You don't have to have a perfectly planned strategy to follow — you just have to make a start and trust yourself to keep putting one foot after the other into the future.

Everything that has happened in your life up to now has been preparing you for this moment, when you launch into a whole new level of achievement and experience. Do this for yourself, and I guarantee you'll be blown away by how incredible your life will become on the other side. Commit to kicking the habits that have held you back in the past, so you can get the competitive edge in your business, fall even more in love with your spouse, raise amazing kids and forever change your family tree.

You finished the book. Now what?

First, if you finished this book, I want to say: congratulations.

The first step to self-improvement begins with awareness and education. By finishing this book, you're well on your way.

Of course, a book might not be enough.

Maybe you need additional resources...

Maybe you need a community of sober entrepreneurs to keep you focused, grounded, and improving...

If you're interested in getting more help, simply go to:

soberentrepreneur.com/bonus

This page will be updated from time to time with resources that are helping me, and that I believe could help you.

You'll also find a way to contact me through that page. And if you're stuck, you should definitely reach out. I know how hard it is to go it alone. Please don't do that to yourself.

Thanks again, and look forward to hearing from you!

- Russ

ACKNOWLEDGEMENTS

First, an insanely huge thank you goes out to Laura Hanly for her patience, dedication, and commitment to me and this concept of a book. I should have hired you first!

Thank you to Garrett J. White and the Wake Up Warrior team. Without your relentless commitment to big ass results, I would not be sharing my story. Much of the conversation around my body, being, balance, and business is interwoven with concepts developed by Wake Up Warrior. I started this book after Garrett allowed the use of these ideas and terms directly, so there will be a future version to marry the concepts cleanly (Garrett – I had to SHIP!).

Mom, you've always been my #1 fan. Thank you for everything you've done. I am here today because of your relentless love and support.

Dad, I love you and I hope you're able to find support and peace within this book.

Thank you to my infinitely loving family: Becky aka "Grace", Billy, Phil, Junko, Grandma Augusta, and many, many more siblings, cousins, aunts, uncles and extended family.

Thank you to my insanely amazing Design Pickle family for allowing me the time and space to focus on this project. You guys keep the lights on and continue to crush it every day.

Thank you to Taylor Pearson, Tim Ferriss, Peter Shankman, Luke Kayyem, Kings 22, Matt Blanton and Chris Ronzio. Your work and drive continues to inspire me.

Thank you to God, for well, you know, everything.

Finally, thank you to the woman of my dreams, my queen, my soulmate, Mika Jennifer Perry. There is no amount of words I could ever write to match the love and patience you have given me. #hearteyes

ABOUT THE AUTHOR

Russ Perry lives with his family in Scottsdale, Arizona. A third-generation Arizona native, he grew up in Tucson, Arizona and graduated from Arizona State University with a degree in design and human communications. A creative at heart, he's consulted for brands such as LG, Coca-Cola, Apple, IKEA, and dozens of amazing and hardworking B2B companies.

When he's not sharing the story you're holding in your hands, he's feverishly working on his two startups:

Design Pickle – The world's #1 flat-rate graphic design company in the world, and

Jar – The best tool for creative teams to manage creative requests.

Learn more about Russ, including his latest work and speaking opportunities, at russperry.co or Instagram and Facebook under / @russperry (and pretty much the first few pages of Google when you search "Russ Perry").

Made in the USA
San Bernardino, CA
17 February 2018